NATURALLY INCLUSIVE

Engaging Children of All Abilities Outdoors

Ruth Wilson, PhD

www.gryphonhouse.com

BULK PURCHASE

Gryphon House books are available for special premiums and sales promotions as well as for fund-raising use. Special editions or book excerpts also can be created to specifications. For details, call 800.638.0928.

DISCLAIMER

Gryphon House, Inc., cannot be held responsible for damage, mishap, or injury incurred during the use of or because of activities in this book. Appropriate and reasonable caution and adult supervision of children involved in activities and corresponding to the age and capability of each child involved are recommended at all times. Do not leave children unattended at any time. Observe safety and caution at all times.

PRAISE

for

Naturally Inclusive:
Engaging Children of All Abilities Outdoors:

❝ What an inspiring book! Ruth Wilson fully explores the great potential of connecting children with special needs to the natural world. In that larger world, every living thing has special abilities, different from those of other individuals within their own species and certainly from those of other species. Nature, then, represents both ultimate diversity and universal shared experience, a sense of belonging within the largest family. And through this awareness comes healing."

—**RICHARD LOUV**, author of *Last Child in the Woods: Saving Our Children from Nature-Deficit Disorder* and *Our Wild Calling: How Connecting with Animals Can Transform Our Lives— And Save Theirs*

❝ In the literature on connecting children with nature, children with special needs are often a forgotten population. This book gives them, their parents, and the people who create inclusive nature-play-and-learning programs overdue attention. Its wisdom reflects Ruth Wilson's decades of work with children in nature and her deep knowledge of relevant research. She weaves advice about how to work with children with a variety of special needs together with evidence about benefits of nature engagement for all children. Her stories about parents, teachers, and children with diverse abilities bring general ideas to life. The result is an essential guide for the creation of inclusive nature-based play spaces and programs, as well as an inspiring resource for connecting every child to nature."

—**LOUISE CHAWLA**, Professor Emerita, Program in Environmental Design, University of Colorado Boulder

❝ I highly recommend this newest book from Dr. Ruth Wilson. It fills an important gap in illuminating how to more effectively serve the needs of all children's healthy development and overall well-being through meaningful experiences with nature

PRAISE

for

Naturally Inclusive:
Engaging Children of All Abilities Outdoors:

in their everyday lives. While solidly grounded in research and practice, Dr. Wilson is also an artful communicator—clear and compelling, innovative and inspiring, positive and practical, hopeful and healing. May the book be read, shared, and applied widely in children's lives!"

—CHERYL CHARLES, PHD, Cofounder and CEO Emerita, Children & Nature Network

❝ A truly fascinating book, this resource offers a comprehensive guide on various nature programs and practices to meet the needs of every child."

—ANGELA HANSCOM, author of *Balanced and Barefoot: How Unrestricted Outdoor Play Makes for Strong, Confident, and Capable Children* and founder of TimberNook, an award-winning nature-based program

❝ [This book] underscores the importance of nature connection for each and every child. Well-researched examples and poignant anecdotes reveal just how fulfilling nature-based learning can be for a child's mind, body, and spirit. This is truly an informative and inspirational read for nature-based educators and parents alike!"

—MONICA WIEDEL-LUBINSKI, Director of the Eastern Region Association of Forest and Nature Schools

Dedication

To my husband,

Frederick Wilson,

who has
supported and inspired me
in so many ways
over our years together.

Naturally Inclusive: Engaging Children of All Abilities Outdoors

TABLE of CONTENTS

Preface

This book is about the beauty of diversity and the importance of inclusion as applied to young children with differing abilities. This book is also about nature as an exemplar of diversity and a catalyst for inclusion.

We see diversity in the natural world around us and recognize this as an indication of a healthy ecosystem. We see diversity in the human community and are sometimes perplexed by the response to such diversity. One unwelcome response takes the form of discrimination and exclusion. People with differing abilities are sometimes discriminated against and find themselves excluded from certain settings, activities, and opportunities, including active engagement with the world of nature. This is troubling and unfortunate, as everyone has a right to nature and can benefit from nature's gifts. People with special needs or differing abilities may benefit even more than others from close connections with nature.

While children with special needs often face physical and social barriers to more intense engagement with the natural world, stories and testimonials generously shared by families, teachers, and therapists indicate that these challenges need not prevent children with disabilities from enjoying the many benefits nature has to offer. Their stories and the focus of this book— while addressing nature connections for children with special needs—are more about abilities and capabilities than disabilities. The focus is on well-being and happiness. The intent of this book is to promote human flourishing, optimal development, and quality of life for young children with differing abilities.

This book is also about inclusion and belonging. Inclusion occurs when people with differing abilities are valued, viewed as contributing members of the group, and feel a sense of belonging. Nature doesn't discriminate or judge. It offers a welcoming environment and serves as a natural habitat for all children. When given the opportunity, many young children experience a sense of kinship with the animals and plants they encounter in natural environments. Just being in nature and with nature can help children with special needs feel accepted and cared for. Nature tells them that they belong and that they are an integral part of something larger than themselves.

Acknowledgments

For the many contributors to this book, I would like to extend my deepest appreciation and gratitude. Your stories and insights have inspired me; I am sure they will inspire the readers as well. For each of you, I am deeply grateful.

Sally Anderson

Patti Bailie

Kathryn Hunt Baker

Marilyn Brink

Laura Brothwell

Lisa Burris

Huan Chen

Sylvia Collazo

Sandra Duncan

Beth Frankel

Carie Green

Misti Guenther

Christine Kiewra

Helen McDonald

Mariam Murphy

Anne Ouwerkerk

Tiffany Pearsall

Jane Piselli

Allyson Rhatigan

Sheila Williams Ridge

Nancy Rosenow

Jennifer Rosinia

Deborah Schein

Patty Born Selly

Marisa Soboleski

Rachel Tenney

Nora Thompson

Angela Wildermuth

Sierra Woosley

Crista Yagjian

Meixi Yan

Xi Yang

Xiuping Yang

Gigi Schroeder Yu

Shiqi Yue

CHAPTER 1

The Role of Nature in Our Lives

"

Our identity is nature—
not concrete and asphalt.

— CLEMENS ARVAY,
author

Nature isn't a frill, nor is it a playground or an amusement park. Nature is a necessity in our lives. We need nature for our very existence, as nature is the source of our food, water, air, and shelter. But nature does far more than provide for our basic physical needs. We tend to be happier, healthier, more socially engaged, and more creative when nature is an integral part of our daily lives. These benefits apply to people of all ages and abilities when they are physically, emotionally, and psychologically connected with nature. Unfortunately, the way many people live today fosters disconnection from the world of nature. This is true for children as well as adults. This introductory chapter focuses on the role of nature in our lives, describes nature-related characteristics in humans, and introduces readers to different terms and concepts about the study of nature and its effects on humans. It also looks at what happens when the role of nature takes a back seat in our everyday life.

Nature—Our Natural Habitat

A *habitat* is the place or environment in which a living being usually lives. The habitat provides the conditions and resources that a being needs to live and thrive. Taken out of its natural habitat, a living creature will experience stress and may even die. Humans, as living beings, have been formed and shaped over millions of years by the natural environment. Nature is a habitat for humans.

Of course, humans have changed and evolved over time. We've created and adapted to different types of environments. Yet, our evolutionary roots—our interconnectedness with nature—remain inside our psyche and bodies. We need nature to maintain our health and well-being.

Children and Nature

The amount of time children spend in our natural habitat has decreased dramatically over the last fifty years, resulting in serious concerns about what Richard Louv, author of *Last Child in the Woods*, refers to as *nature-deficit disorder*. While this term is not intended to represent a medical diagnosis, it does call attention to physical, emotional, and social concerns related to the human costs of alienation from nature. These costs, as outlined by Louv, include the following:

- ✿ Diminished use of the senses
- ✿ Attention difficulties
- ✿ Higher rates of physical illnesses
- ✿ Higher rates of mental illnesses

Families, educators, researchers, youth leaders, health-care providers, landscape architects, psychologists, and many others are beginning to take notice of the outcomes of diminishing interactions between children and nature.

As interaction with nature diminishes, so, too, do understandings and appreciation of the natural world. People often fear what they don't understand. Fear and dislike of natural things is called *biophobia*, which not only reduces the motivation to protect wildlife and other forms of nature but also further discourages direct contact with nature. People who don't like nature aren't inclined to spend time engaged with it. This comes at a cost, not only to the environment but to ourselves. According to E.O. Wilson, on the other hand, humans have an innate affinity for the natural world, which he calls *biophilia*. He and his colleagues proposed that biophilia is biologically based and integral to the holistic development of humans.

The benefits to human health and well-being by engaging with nature are too great to be dismissed or ignored (Putra et al., 2020). While such benefits apply to all ages and abilities, the importance of nature connection may be especially consequential during the early years and may be more impactful for children with special needs than for other children (Faber Taylor, Kuo, and Sullivan, 2001; Byström, Grahn, and Hägerhäll, 2019; Galbraith and Lancaster, 2020).

Nature excites, challenges, motivates, and brings joy to children. Yet, children with special needs tend to visit green space less often than typically developing children (Horton, 2017). Children with special needs often face physical, emotional, and social barriers to more intense engagement with nature, but these barriers need not prevent them from experiencing nature. Throughout this book, we will take a look at ways to get around these barriers.

Human beings, regardless of age, culture, or ability, share the capability to develop. Researcher Louise Chawla says that this capability is part of what it means to be human. In her 2015 article "Benefits of Nature Contact for Children," Chawla lists ways in which access to nature enables children to realize what are referred to as *central capabilities*. These capabilities include the following:

- A normal lifespan and good health
- The ability to move from place to place
- The ability to use their senses and experience pleasure
- Opportunities to use their imaginations
- Opportunities to think and reason
- Attachment to things and people outside themselves
- Recognizing and showing concern for other human beings, animals, plants, and the world of natures
- Opportunities to laugh and play

Nature connectedness is a basic human need that, when met, promotes health, development, and well-being. On the other hand, when this need is not fulfilled, humans suffer ill effects physically, emotionally, psychologically, and even socially.

Clemens Arvay is a prominent researcher in eco-psychosomatics, the study of the mental and physical effects of nature on humans. He explains how this field views humans as part of the network of life and how related research focuses on the close connection between mind, body, and nature, which everyone needs for optimal physical, social, and emotional development.

His book *Nature and Autism Spectrum Disorder: Supporting the Development of Autistic Children through Biodiversity* (2021) focuses specifically on children with autism spectrum disorder (ASD). Researchers are not the only ones who recognize the importance of nature on humans. Families of all children, including those with special needs, also see the positive benefits of the natural habitat on their own children as illustrated in the following vignette.

> Weston's mom, Misti, describes him as "a kid with high sensory needs and a barrel for a body." She explains how he "crashes into furniture and constantly tests his strength on toys, trees, sticks, the ground, and sometimes on other humans. . . . His brain seems to be moving so fast, and his head at times seems to have a hard time syncing with his body."
>
> Weston also loves the outdoors. Misti refers to the natural environment as Weston's natural habitat, as this is where he is most himself. His favorite thing to do outdoors is to play with his friends. "It's when he's outdoors that Weston is most patient with other kids. He'll take on the role of organizer. He'll plan activities and make up games. But it's different indoors. It seems as if the walls are closing in on him. At times, Weston gets overstimulated, and that's when bad decisions happen. Weston might respond with anger; he might start hitting people and things."
>
> Misti thinks that Weston's demeanor and behaviors are different outdoors due, in part, to the sense of freedom he experiences there. "There are fewer constraints, fewer have-to's. Outdoors, Weston isn't coaxed into one way of doing things. He can make his own path."
>
> Weston is a six-year-old who attended SOL Forest School in Tijeras, New Mexico, before his family moved to California. The forest gave him the space and freedom to engage deeply with nature. This sense of freedom seemed to fit Weston well. Misti described this as "the forest giving him a place to play out his thoughts, with no barriers to make him feel trapped."
>
> Misti sees Weston at his best when he can spend at least four hours outdoors during the day. "He'd spend all day outdoors if he could. Outdoors, he has no concept of time. He's so engulfed in what he's doing."

Based on the facts that nature is something we all need and that biophilia is something we all have or can quickly develop, we can be assured that providing rich opportunities for children to be deeply engaged with nature is an effective way to promote their overall health and well-being.

While the term *biophilia* may be new to some people, the meaning may reside deep in our bones. After being introduced to the term, Helen McDonald, Pedagogical Director of the Collaborative Teachers Institute in New Mexico, said, "I think I have been looking for that word—*biophilia*—for my whole adult life." She went on to say that the opportunity to spend time outside "should really be considered a basic human right." Helen's idea about access to nature as a basic human right is reflected in *Home to Us All: How Connecting with Nature Helps Us Care for Ourselves and the Earth,* a report developed by Cheryl Charles and colleagues from the Children & Nature Network (www.childrenandnature.org) and the #Nature for All movement (http://natureforall.global/).

This report emphasizes the importance of opportunities for children to experience the many facets of the natural world at an early age. One of the related goals of #Nature for All is to "inspire opportunities for all people to experience and connect meaningfully with nature." Achieving this goal requires, among many other considerations, attention to the special needs of children with disabilities.

Naturalistic Intelligence

In addition to biophilia, *naturalistic intelligence* is another nature-related characteristic found in humans. Howard Gardner, a developmental psychologist, suggests that human intelligence isn't limited to what is generally measured on IQ tests. Instead, he says that humans have what he calls "multiple intelligences." In *Frames of Mind: The Theory of Multiple Intelligences* (1983), Gardner proposes eight abilities that manifest multiple intelligences:

- ✿ Linguistic
- ✿ Musical

RESEARCH NOTE:
NATURE MATTERS TO CHILDREN

In a study of young children's views on what matters to them, researchers invited a group of preschool children with and without special needs to draw the activities and objects they liked and viewed as "good" in their school setting. Then, the children were asked to talk about their drawings and to share what they liked and didn't like about their school experiences (Lundqvist, Allodi, and Siljehag, 2019).

The researchers interpreted the children's expressions of positive and negative experiences and their indications of what mattered to them as their "needs and values." The children's responses included a long list of needs and values:

- A sense of belonging with peers
- Opportunities for play, creative activities, and thinking
- Experiences of speed, excitement, and physical challenges
- Elements of coziness, withdrawal, and comfort for recreation
- Feeling safe
- Experiences of growth in knowledge and understanding of the world
- Feelings of freedom and autonomy
- Comforting objects and bonds with home and family
- Connection with nature

Specifically, children said they enjoyed green grass, yellow suns, blue clouds, skies, big green trees with leaves, branches, apples, raindrops, stones, forests, sand, snow, rainbows, brown earth, moons and stars, and birds. Almost all the children indicated that they liked to play outdoors and that they preferred playing in a natural environment to playing in a playground with traditional equipment.

While the preschoolers described their outdoor and nature-related activities as fun and interesting, the researchers also noted how such activities related to self-determination, especially in the areas of autonomy, relatedness, and competence. The researchers highlighted ways in which experiences with nature can have a positive effect on children's development and well-being. They also noted the importance of outdoor play in addressing the needs and values of both typically developing children and children with special needs. For example, they described how some children might value and need more exciting and challenging activities, while other children might value and need more elements of coziness and opportunities for withdrawal.

- Logical-mathematical
- Spatial
- Bodily-kinesthetic
- Interpersonal
- Intrapersonal
- Naturalistic

The naturalistic intelligence is sometimes referred to as "nature smart," as it reflects an understanding of nature. While naturalistic intelligence includes the ability to recognize plants, animals, and other parts of the natural environment, it also includes the ability to make connections with elements in the natural world. For the naturalistic intelligence to thrive, children need frequent, positive experiences with nature.

While everyone can benefit from engagement with nature, the benefits of such engagement may be greater for individuals with ASD. Angela Wildermuth, founder, director, and lead teacher of Wilderkids Urban Forest School in St. Louis, Missouri, had firsthand experience of how one child with ASD benefited from this engagement with nature.

Steven looked a lot like every other child I had in my nature program at his age—unique, imaginative, and so precious. He's six years old now, but I've known him since he was three. For the first year or so, I wasn't aware of the fact that he had any diagnosis of special needs. I know now that he is on the autism spectrum. Steven attended my once-per-week forest school one year and attended a summer camp I ran for two summers. I believe Steven enjoyed the outdoor programs so much because—like all the other children who came—he experienced an emotional acceptance and support needed to engage deeply in the special type of play that nature offers him, amidst a community of others.

It may have been harder for Steven to make emotional connections with other people, but I don't believe this affected his ability to connect to nature. He displayed an intensity to his imaginative play in nature that was unmatched by almost any other child I've seen. Steven could be deeply focused and concentrating, despite lots of other activities going on around him. He would zone in on one or two particular loose parts that called to him—a stick, a few boards, or a piece of trash—to build something creative, such as a robot, a spaceship, or a new type of mechanical apparatus.

Being in nature with open-ended playthings gave Steven the chance to take ownership of natural objects that were, in essence, up for grabs. If Steven found something and imagined what that something was—for instance a board being a robot—then, to him, it *was* a robot. If someone came by and said, "That's a cool board you found!" he would angrily tell them "It's NOT a board! It's a ROBOT!"

One week at summer camp, bald cypress boughs had been scattered around the grass after a storm. Like many children, Steven gravitated toward the big sticks—grabbing them, trailing them behind him for later use, or assembling them together. After disengaging from the main group for a while, Steven was soon joined by another child who hadn't been particularly

drawn to play with him before. I think his intense and thoughtful style intrigued some of his peers and enticed them to try his style, too.

Steven's imaginative style seemed to make it easier for kids to engage with him—but only as long as they accepted the parameters he established. Only after they entered *his* imaginary world would Steven allow them to offer suggestions or modifications. In many ways, the extent to which Steven could connect to nature seemed only inhibited by the extent to which others could imagine.

One day at camp as the children were frolicking in the creek, Steven scooped up a handful of wet sand from the shallow bottom and convincingly shouted, "Look guys, it's a sand slug!" I had to think hard about whether or not sand slugs actually lived in our locale. Steven repeated his announcement until some other children came to look. Whether the "sand slug" in his hands was real or not remained a fleeting mystery. The difference between the real and the unreal in this case was delightfully unclear and magically welcomed. I only wonder how much more magic and possibilities Steven will create, discover, and share throughout his lifetime.

Nature's Contribution to Quality of Life

Quality of life, as defined by the World Health Organization, is an individual's "perception of their position in life, in the context of the culture and value systems in which they live and in relation to their goals, expectations, standards and concerns." As this definition indicates, quality of life clearly means more than the simple absence of discomfort, illness, or trauma. Quality of life is a presence, an overall feeling of well-being encompassing the physical, psychological, and social aspects of one's life, including the following:

- ❀ Interpersonal relations
- ❀ Social inclusion
- ❀ Personal development
- ❀ Physical well-being

- ❀ Self-determination
- ❀ Material well-being
- ❀ Emotional well-being
- ❀ Human and legal rights

Quality of life can also include the extent to which an individual is *satisfied* with various domains of his or her own life; this is the subjective quality of life. It's important for interventions or treatments for people with special needs to include a focus on subjective quality of life—how the individual perceives her life, not just what others think would be a good quality of life for that person.

An enhanced quality of life is a realistic and obtainable goal for all persons, including people with special needs. Research conducted over the past several decades supports the idea that engagement with nature can play a significant role in promoting subjective quality of life. For example, a team of researchers from four different countries found that people with more frequent and intense engagement with nature tend to be happier, healthier, and more creative than people who spend little time engaged with nature (Hartig et al., 2014). Another group of researchers found that **exposure to green space may potentially increase prosocial behavior,** such as offering help, sharing, cooperating, and comforting, **among children and adolescents** (Putra et al., 2020). Further research identified a list of twenty evidence-based health benefits of nature contact, including physical and mental health, social well-being, and happiness (Frumkin et al., 2017). These findings of specific benefits attest to the value of nature engagement for enhancing quality of life.

Kinship

Humans, like all other living things, are social beings. We live in relationship with other humans and with the rest of the natural world. Kinship is an integral part of this reality. While the natural world is our natural habitat, it's more than the place where we live.

The concept of nature as a contributor to our quality of life focuses on relationships, connectedness, and even kinship. Kinship, in some contexts, refers to a physical relationship, as in a blood relationship. But kinship can also be experienced as an emotional relationship. We sometimes refer to this as having emotional ties. It's not unusual to see expressions of such emotional ties in children's spontaneous interactions with elements of nature. Children readily talk to animals, express concern for an animal or plant in distress, and seek comfort in the branches of a tree.

Kinship with nature is rooted in meaning and a meaning-oriented relationship. It's reflected in the recognition that the world in which we live is a common world—a world to be shared by all other creatures. This recognition is crucial to a child's—and society's—holistic development. This topic is developed in more detail in chapter 7.

A kinship relationship between humans and the rest of nature is grounded in a biological understanding of the natural world. All species are descended from a single ancestral population. This makes all other species our kin. We—humans and other-than-humans—are inhabitants of each other's worlds. According to some researchers, sense of kinship with nature is vital for the health and well-being of children and the natural environment (Giusti et al., 2018).

Heather Fox and colleagues developed an Children's Environmental Kinship Framework (2020), a framework for learning about, in, with, and for the whole of the natural world. The guide is designed to inspire curriculum, provide a framework for documenting related learning, and encourage new practices in nature-based education. As an extension of this effort, the authors of the guide also formed Environmental Kinship International (EKI) to support this vision more broadly. EKI's central tenet is that time spent with nature experiencing and celebrating diversity and interdependence helps strengthen our pre-existing kinship with the natural world. You can learn more about the guide at https://www.environmentalkinship.org/

Shifts in Thinking about the Natural World

Some philosophical, psychological, and religious belief systems—especially prominent in the Western dominant culture—perpetuate the idea that humans are separate from and superior to the rest of the natural world. This way of thinking—sometimes referred to as *anthropocentrism*—is being challenged by scholars from different disciplines.

COMMON WORLDS

The *common worlds* concept is an inclusive idea that recognizes humans as beings in common with other species and elements of the natural world. The focus is on coexistence in the world with others. This perspective helps us avoid the divisive distinction often drawn between human societies and natural environments. It sees human lives as being situated within an indivisible common worlds, a world shared and entangled with other living beings, nonliving entities, natural forces, and landforms. For more information about the *common worlds* concept, see the Commons Worlds Research Collective website (https://commonworlds.net).

POST-HUMANISM

Post-humanism is also an inclusive idea. It focuses on multiple species sharing one common world. The post-human perspective helps us avoid assumptions based on the belief that humans are superior to the rest of the natural world. Post-humanism focuses on the interdependence between humans and the more-than-human world.

CHILDHOODNATURE

Childhoodnature is based on the understanding that children *are* nature and that meaning making occurs as children and nature work together. The childhoodnature concept rejects a human-centered view of nature, which considers humans the most significant entity on Earth. Instead, the childhoodnature perspective recognizes that we are part of nature, and it encourages mutually healthy relationships. You can find more information about childhoodnature through the Childhoodnature Collective website (www.childhoodnature.com) and from *Research Handbook on Childhoodnature* (Cutter-Mackenzie-Knowles, Malone, and Hacking, 2020).

Each of these terms reflect in some way the idea of "kinship with" versus "dominion over" nature. Included in these concepts is a rejection of the idea that humans are separate from and/or superior to the rest of nature. These concepts reflect eco-centric (nature-centered) versus anthropocentric (human-centered) worldviews.

The common worlds, post-humanism, and childhoodnature concepts have important implications for strengthening connections between children and nature. This book explores these implications in later chapters:

- ❀ Nature as teacher (chapter 4)
- ❀ Nature as healer (chapter 5)
- ❀ Nature as play partner (chapter 6)
- ❀ Nature for holistic development (chapter 7)

I've also embedded these implications in the suggestions offered on how to connect children with animals (chapter 9) and plants (chapter 10). The inclusiveness embedded in these perspectives may pave the way for—or reinforce—a different way of thinking about children with special needs.

As discussed in the next chapter, there's a tendency to view children as being either "typically developing" or "special needs." While this categorization may be helpful in some ways, it can also lead to missing the larger picture—recognizing that all children share certain characteristics and certain needs, including deep engagement with nature. Moving beyond the tendency to think and act in dualistic terms—as in humans/nature and typically developing/special needs—may usher in a more inclusive view of what constitutes a healthy society. This more inclusive view rejects the concepts of what is "normal" and the superiority of humans over nature. It emphasizes, instead, common worlds where all can thrive.

REFERENCES

Arvay, Clemens G. 2021. *Nature and Autism Spectrum Disorder: Supporting the Development of Autistic Children through Biodiversity.* Abingdon-on-Thames, Oxfordshire, England, UK: Routledge.

Byström, Kristina, Patrik Grahn, and Caroline Hägerhäll. 2019. "Vitality from Experiences in Nature and Contact with Animals—A Way to Develop Joint Attention and Social Engagement in Children with Autism?" *International Journal of Environmental Research and Public Health* 16(23): 4673.

Charles, Cheryl, et al. 2018. *Home to Us All: How Connecting with Nature Helps Us Care for Ourselves and the Earth.* Minneapolis, MN: Children & Nature Network.

Chawla, Louise. 2015. "Benefits of Nature Contact for Children." *Journal of Planning Literature* 30(4): 433–452.

Cutter-Mackenzie-Knowles, Amy, Karen Malone, and Elisabeth Barratt Hacking, eds. 2020. *Research Handbook on Childhoodnature.* New York: Springer.

Faber Taylor, Andrea, Frances E. Kuo, and William C. Sullivan. 2001. "Coping with ADD: The Surprising Connection to Green Play Settings." *Environment and Behavior* 33(1): 54–77.

Fox, Heather, et al. 2020. Children's Environmental Kinship Framework. https://www.environmentalkinship.org/

Frumkin, Howard, et al. 2017. "Nature Contact and Human Health: A Research Agenda." *Environmental Health Perspectives* 125(7). https://doi.org/10.1289/EHP1663

Galbraith, Carolyn, and Julie Lancaster. 2020. "Children with Autism in Wild Nature: Exploring Australian Parent Perceptions Using Photovoice." *Journal of Outdoor and Environmental Education* 23: 293–307.

Gardner, Howard. 1983. *Frames of Mind: The Theory of Multiple Intelligences.* New York: Basic Books.

Giusti, Matteo, et al. 2018. "A Framework to Assess Where and How Children Connect to Nature." *Frontiers in Psychology* 8: 2283.

Hartig, Terry, et al. 2014. "Nature and Health." *Annual Review of Public Health* 35: 207–228.

Horton, John. 2017. "Disabilities, Urban Natures, and Children's Outdoor Play." *Social and Cultural Geography* 18(8): 1152–1174.

Louv, Richard. 2008. *Last Child in the Woods: Saving Our Children from Nature-Deficit Disorder.* Chapel Hill, NC: Algonquin Books

Lundqvist, Johanna, Mara W. Allodi, and Eva Siljehag. 2019. "Values and Needs of Children with and without Special Educational Needs in Early School Years: A Study of Young Children's Views on What Matters to Them." *Scandinavian Journal of Educational Research* 63(6): 951–967.

Putra, I Gusti Ngurah Edi, et al. 2020. "The Relationship between Green Space and Prosocial Behaviour among Children and Adolescents: A Systematic Review." *Frontiers in Psychology* 11: 859.

Wilson, Edward O. 1984. *Biophilia.* Cambridge, MA: Harvard University Press.

CHAPTER 2

Nature and Young Children with Special Needs

> **"**
>
> Now I see the secret of the making of the best person.
> It is to grow in the open air and to eat
> and sleep with the earth.
>
> — WALT WHITMAN,
> "Song of the Open Road, 6"

"I'm different, not less"—that's how Dr. Temple Grandin describes herself as a person with autism (Grandin, 2020). This statement can be used in reference to all people with special needs. People with disabilities have certain conditions or characteristics that differ from what we may refer to as "normal" or "typical." Being "out of the norm," however, does not make a person "less than" people within the norm.

It's not unusual for teachers to refer to the children in their class as being either "typically developing" or "special needs." While these designations aren't necessarily harmful in themselves, they do call attention to differences. If you're not "typically developing," some of your characteristics or some aspects of your development differ from the norm. Unfortunately, "the norm" is often used as the measuring stick as to what is most desirable. This idea needs to be challenged. Rather than looking to the norm as to what is better, we should be looking to the unique gifts possessed by each person. Every child is able bodied: every child has abilities, gifts, and strengths.

Rather than making a "normal life" the goal of intervention, it would be better to focus on quality of life and the gifts each child brings to his own life and the lives around them.

This chapter focuses on how nature exposure and nature engagement can help children with differing abilities experience quality of life. Related discussion focuses on how nature-based interventions and nature-rich environments can promote inclusion and positive social interactions. I also offer suggestions on how to make nature engagement more accessible for children with different types of disabilities. Highlighted throughout the discussion is the importance of inclusion and attention to what children like, want, and respond to.

Quality of Life for Children with Special Needs

As stated in chapter 1, quality of life means more than the absence of discomfort, illness, or trauma. Subjective quality of life, based on the individual's perceptions and evaluations, is a life of joy, contentment, and satisfaction. Marilyn Brink, an early childhood specialist and trainer for NatureStart professional development in Brookfield, Illinois, describes one such experience in which a family's visit to a rainy beach does not result in disappointment.

> A family from Wisconsin decided to celebrate one of their children's birthdays by spending a weekend camping in a state park not far from their home. They liked this particular park because it had a lake and accessibility-mat pathways allowing for wheelchair access to the lake. One of the children has severe developmental and physical disabilities and depends on a wheelchair for mobility.
>
> The mother had recently attended a professional workshop on the benefits of nature for children, and she was eager to spend time outdoors with her family. But it was rainy the weekend they went camping. Ordinarily, she would have suggested staying inside the camper,

as the weather was often the determinant for whether or not they could easily get their son outdoors in his wheelchair. Because it was a light rainfall, there weren't many people at the beach, so she decided to take all the children. She used the accessibility mat to move their son to the water. Once there, she lifted him out of his wheelchair and seated him on the sandy bottom of the lake in water up to his waist. His response reflected great joy. He was so happy and excited to be in the water! Playing in the lake in the rain with his family would certainly be cherished as a memorable experience! The family would look back on this day as a day that was "really good."

Families with children with special needs are not the only ones who recognize the positive influence of nature on the quality of life. In the Program Spotlight box on page 16, two early childhood educators describe how the quality of life improves for children with and without special needs in their nature-based programs.

Program Spotlight box on page 16

RESEARCH NOTE:
QUALITY OF LIFE FOR YOUNG CHILDREN

Researchers might define *quality of life* in terms of well-being. A child, however, might describe it as "life that is really good." Researchers Patricia Barfield and Martha Dreissnack (2018) used the more child-friendly term to ask twenty children with attention-deficit/hyperactivity disorder (ADHD) to describe a time in their life that was really good for them. The children, ages seven to eleven, drew pictures about that time and then talked about what they had drawn. Ninety percent of the children described engaging in some form of activity—often outdoors—and with others. Eighty-five percent referenced nature, and 65 percent referenced relational connections.

These findings suggest that the focus of intervention for children with ADHD should include the three elements that made the children's lives "really good": activities, nature, and connections. Doing so would help move interventions for children with special needs from symptom mitigation to the promotion of life satisfaction. Some examples of interventions or initiatives combining activities, nature, and connections include family nature clubs and the greening of schoolyards.

Scholars conducting this research note how the responses of the children about what makes life really good highlight the restorative effects of nature and reinforce the concept of biophilia. They also suggest that, while biophilia may apply to all children, the implications and/or impact of this natural affinity may be especially important for children with ADHD.

Researchers Francesca Di Carmine and Rita Berto (2020) have found that contact with nature helps children with ADHD cope with their symptoms. Children with ADHD tend to be more attentive and engaged in outdoor activities than they are with indoor activities. They are better able to concentrate after contact with nature, and they tend to score higher on tests of concentration and self-discipline. Some studies included in Di Carmine and Berto's review even indicate that spending time outdoors during preschool protects against developing ADHD in the future.

PLAY FRONTIER*

Play Frontier is a small, nonprofit, nature-based school that serves children ages birth through five in rural Washington. Nature connections are natural for children attending this school, as it's located in the Gifford Pinchot National Forest. Nature adventures are a part of the day for every child enrolled in the program.

Play Frontier was founded on the belief that children need a space to be fully accepted for exactly who they are. Founder Tiffany Pearsall worked with the public school system in making the school an approved site for serving children with special needs. A group of retired forest service employees volunteered their time and expertise in making one of the favorite nearby trails Americans with Disabilities Act (ADA) accessible.

Tiffany is eager to share ideas about the role of nature in meeting the needs of all young children, including those with special needs: "Nature gives children the space and freedom to do what their bodies tell them to do. You don't have to curate the environment, and you don't have to tell children what to do. Nature invites whole-body engagement. It provides a full sensory experience in ways an indoor environment can never do."

"Play and nature is how we learn," she says. This, as Tiffany explains it, applies to people of all ages and abilities. "Nature is a natural equalizer. Everyone experiences the wetness of the creek, the warmth of the sun. For some children, running and splashing in water is what nature invites them to do. Other children work at keeping their socks from getting wet."

Children develop friendships in the forest. While the forest itself is a friend, peers are also more likely to be friends to each other while outdoors, through shared interests and challenges, than they are in the classroom. A child discovers a toad and wants to show it to others. A child wants to build a fort or a den; other children want to get involved. A child tries to climb over a log; another child lends a hand.

Tiffany talks about nature as a teacher: "Nature teaches children how to take care of their own bodies and gear. Learning how to take care of their own coats and boots, for example, helps the children become more independent." Nature also helps children meet individual goals, some set by the children themselves and others listed on a child's individualized education plan (IEP). For example, learning to navigate over uneven surfaces may be an IEP goal for a child with mobility challenges. The forest environment provides plenty of motivation to develop this skill.

Tiffany also describes nature as a healer: "Children experience a sense of calm in the forest; what they observe in nature is comforting. As they visit the same places over time, children see that the leaves are still growing on the trees, the water in the creek is still flowing, and the ants are still moving about. Children are also free of artificial constraints while exploring and playing in the forest. They can run and scream. They can call out to a teacher or peer and get an answer, even when they can't see that person because he or she is around the bend or behind a bush. The children can play with what they find, and there's plenty for everyone." Tiffany describes such experiences as empowering for the children. The children may be tired and hungry after several hours of strenuous activities in the forest, but knowing that they just did something awesome fills them with a sense of accomplishment.

*Based on personal correspondence with Tiffany Pearsall

Benefits of Nature-Based Interventions for Social-Interaction Issues

Difficulties in *social reciprocity*—the back-and-forth flow of social interaction—and communication challenges contribute to a lower quality of life for many people with disabilities. People involved in social reciprocity work together and make adjustments to achieve successful interactions. We see this in action when the behavior of one person influences and is influenced by the behavior of another person. Children with some types of disabilities struggle to show interest in interacting with others or to exchange greetings and smiles. They may prefer solitary activities and avoid social interactions. Jane Piselli, an educator at the New Canaan Nature Center in New Canaan, Connecticut, describes the social-interaction issues one child faced and how nature helped address them.

Under the grandmother pines at the New Canaan Nature Center, three-year-old Robin held out a leaf to a teacher standing near the thicket and said definitively, "It's a bird! I'm going to feed this bird." As another child approached, the teacher stepped back to remove the adult energy from the interaction. The other child looked at Robin, who held out the leaf and definitively stated again, "It's a bird!"

The other child responded, "No, it's a leaf."

A look of confusion broke across Robin's face, as she was sure that she had just cracked the social code of imaginary play; yet, here she was confronted by a child rooted in a moment of reality.

The teacher stepped back into the situation and provided some scaffolding: "Right now, Robin is pretending that the leaf is a bird. Would you like to help Robin feed the bird?" With this explanation, the play relaxed and the other child slipped into the imaginary world that Robin had worked so hard to find.

From the age of two, when Robin first entered the preschool program, teachers noticed that during forest free play, she would sit off to the side observing and watching or would engage children randomly in wrestling games without regard to whether or not they wanted to play roughly. As other children began moving out of parallel play and into cooperative imaginary play, Robin was struggling to understand what imaginary play was, let alone get involved in it. Robin often watched with a quizzical gaze as other children pretended to cook or rescue someone in trouble or adventure to far-off lands. She held strongly to the daily routines and found it difficult whenever the schedule changed. An early intervention specialist who worked closely with the teachers noted that Robin was beginning to show signs of ASD.

With proper scaffolding for her social-emotional learning, Robin's play skills expanded over time in a way her teachers describe as beautiful. Robin now invites other children to engage in friendly imaginary play, and after asking, "Can I play with you?" she confidently joins another group in their imaginary-play scenarios.

Outdoor school provides an abundance of authentic opportunities for social-emotional learning. With smaller class sizes, teachers can closely watch and scaffold play with other children. Natural spaces open up so easily for imaginary play. Children are free to create a world of their own, often by engaging in authentic conversations with each other. Children readily enter this space with confident creativity and a spirit of collaboration. While these skills are important for all children, they take on even greater significance for children still struggling with creative play, especially if they are also challenged by ASD.

The preschool at the New Canaan Nature Center that Robin attends focuses on creating an awareness of, and an appreciation for, the natural world. This unique preschool promotes environmental-education goals while addressing the whole child's developmental needs. Environmental and nature-based education aren't add-ons to the curriculum. They're integral to every aspect of it—including language and literacy, math, art, music, and dramatic play.

The preschool teachers and staff understand the importance of child-driven play in a natural environment. They know that they can aid a child's development but not construct it. They offer aid only when needed. This approach allows children—including children with ASD and other special needs—to construct new understandings about social structure and interactions in more authentic ways.

Without social-reciprocity skills, it's difficult to make and maintain friends; yet, having friends is an important contributor to quality of life. For people with special needs, friendship problems tend to be a lifelong concern. Some interventions can minimize this concern for young children with special needs; for example, nature-based therapies such as animal-assisted therapy (AAT), horticultural (plant-based) therapy, and nature-play therapy can be effective. We will discuss these therapies in later chapters.

A school in England that serves young children ages four to eleven with serious emotional and behavioral concerns added a once-a-week forest-school experience to its intervention program several years ago (Tiplady and Menter 2020). Typical activities during a forest school day included building dens, erecting and using hammocks, climbing trees, building fires and cooking, woodworking, arts and crafts, games, and nature exploration. (Forest schools are described in more detail in chapter 3 on pages 39–40.)

A researcher working with the school observed the students and interviewed staff and families over the academic year and found that the program helped increase the children's engagement and enjoyment and improved their relationships and interactions with others. The teachers noted that, at the beginning of the project, the students typically found social interactions difficult, with group activities often ending in confrontation. Teachers also reported that initially many of the students would choose to engage in their own activities, often with one-on-one adult support. Over the school year, students began to interact more with their peers and relied less on adult support.

The students also developed skills in communication and negotiation and visibly enjoyed their time with one another.

Nature-Rich Environments as Inclusive Environments

While children with special needs face real challenges in navigating their physical and social environments, limiting their involvement in everyday activities may not be in their best interests.

Many typically developing young children's lives are rich in informal nature-related activities, such as raking leaves, splashing water, and digging in sand. Carl Dunst, known for his work in early intervention and early childhood special education, points out that children with disabilities or delays tend to have fewer learning opportunities in community activities than children without disabilities or delays (2020). This may be due, in part, to early intervention and preschool special education practitioners'—as well as families'—viewing formal, structured activities as more important sources of learning than informal, unstructured activities.

───────────────────
PROGRAM SPOTLIGHT:
THE SHIRLEY G. MOORE LABORATORY SCHOOL*

The Shirley G. Moore Laboratory School at the University of Minnesota offers an inclusive, play-based environment for young children ages two to five. When Nell entered my classroom, she had specific needs that I didn't have any experience supporting; neither did my coteacher. Before Nell's arrival, we learned more about those needs and were a little nervous about how she would navigate the social and physical environment, indoors and out. Her family offered to have a personal care assistant with us each day, and we happily obliged. Nell came each day happy to join the class and quickly learned the routine. She was nonverbal but made sounds and gestures that the children and adults in the classroom learned to read very quickly. As winter approached, her physical needs became more obvious. Navigating deep snow, hills, and slippery patches offered challenges but also immense opportunities. We carefully considered the health and safety implications of her navigation and took a sled everywhere we went, just in case she needed some assistance or a rest along the way. When Nell would lose her glasses in a snowy pile, everyone pitched in to help, and her glasses were only broken a few times! Her social skills blossomed during this time. Nell learned to rely on her classmates, and her classmates learned how to be a friend. By the spring, the snow melted, Nell continued to grow, and her personal assistant became less necessary. She started to attend school without the support of an aide and continued to flourish through that school year and the next. Her family was able to choose an inclusive kindergarten for her in the school district, and they occasionally still reach out to us and thank us for the gift of her nature-based experiences in preschool and note them as a pivotal moment in her development, especially socially.

*Contributed by Sheila Williams Ridge, MA, Director, Shirley G. Moore Laboratory School, University of Minnesota

Dunst (2020) highlights the importance of informal activities for young children with disabilities, suggesting that families, caregivers, and educators pay attention to the settings in which children

PROGRAM SPOTLIGHT
STONE HEN*

In 2018, Laura Brothwell founded Stone Hen Childcare in North Lincolnshire, United Kingdom, with the goal of providing children with an environment that would fuel their passion for learning and support their holistic development. She wanted Stone Hen to embrace the magic of nature-based, child-led learning in a setting away from the pressures and strain of modern life.

Laura chose the name "Stone Hen" to reflect the architectural wall outside the setting, which features three pillars and a railing, with a stone hen sitting on each of the pillars. Laura's family placed the stone hens there in appreciation of the magic they had experienced in raising chickens over many years. Laura wanted to share some of that magic with the children, ranging in age from six months to four years, who attend Stone Hen.

The children spend most of their time experiencing the freedom and possibilities offered through immersion in nature. The outdoor environment includes a water source, trees, bird tables, a pond, frog and fairy gardens, a mud kitchen, and animal enclosures. Frequent adventures into the surrounding woodlands, fields, canals, rivers, fishing ponds, and parks are also a part of the experience.

Some of the children enrolled at Stone Hen have diagnosed disabilities and special educational needs; Andrew is one such child. Andrew entered Stone Hen at the age of twenty-two months with virtually no spoken language. The staff soon noticed major differences in how Andrew responded to indoor and outdoor experiences. Indoors, he usually distanced himself from others and made few attempts to communicate. The one activity he seemed to enjoy indoors was emptying flowerpots and playing with the soil. Outdoors, Andrew loves digging in the earth and searching for tiny organisms. His close observations and focused investigations often attract the curious attention of others. He still uses limited verbal communication, but Andrew welcomes the involvement of other children in his outdoor explorations.

Andrew likes to roam free in the woodlands near Stone Hen, and his teachers are generally comfortable with letting him do so.

continued on page 21

spend their time, identify and attend to child interests and how interesting the activities are, and consider the role they play in promoting child participation in nature-related activities.

According to Dunst, some settings offer more affordances for child-initiated activity than others. *Affordance* refers to the characteristics and features of a setting or environment that invite child engagement and interaction. For example, a child may see a tree with low branches and perceive it as an opportunity for climbing. Water invites splashing, and sand invites digging.

Nature is nondiscriminatory, and nature-based activities invite differing forms of interaction. With nature as an integrating context—or nature as the teacher—one activity can accommodate different interests and skill levels. Gardening is an excellent example of an inclusive and multilevel activity. While some children will do well in digging earth and planting seeds, others might be measuring the dimensions of the garden or recording dates when certain seeds are planted and seedlings first appear. In addition to being a multilevel activity, gardening can also promote all areas of learning and development.

Raised-bed gardens can make gardening more accessible for some young children. While this is especially important for children in wheelchairs, other children may also benefit. Raised beds let children stand rather than kneel, which may help a child exercise more control over fine motor movements required for planting, weeding, and watering. Raised beds place gardening tasks at a more comfortable eye level for some children, and they may help a child with balance problems, too. In planning raised-bed gardens, consider height requirements for children in wheelchairs, comfortable heights for children as they stand, and space requirements for maneuvering around beds. The book *Gardening for Children with Autism Spectrum Disorders and Special Educational Needs: Engaging with Nature to Combat Anxiety, Promote Sensory Integration, and Build Social Skills* by Natasha Etherington offers useful information on how to create a simple gardening

continued from page 20

He seems to have self-awareness about his abilities in relation to potential risks, and he's also learned how to ask for help when needed. He is one of the most adept of the younger children in preparing himself to go outdoors: he shows remarkable patience and independence in donning a coat, hat, and boots. Andrew has demonstrated a special knack for foraging in berry bushes and gardens. He's learned how to wash the food before eating it and often shares what he has with others.

Andrew's parents always knew that he loved nature and that he was calmer and more attentive when outdoors; yet they were amazed when they observed him at Stone Hen interacting with other children and watching other children seek him out as a play partner.

Laura has observed similar growth in communication and social-interaction skills of other children with special educational needs. Several of the children in her program also attend a public-school intervention program for young children with disabilities. Teachers and therapists from the public-school program, after visiting Stone Hen, remarked on how some of their students seemed like different children when they were playing and interacting in the natural environment. One child even demonstrated more independent mobility skills. In the public-school setting, he uses a walking support device, but at Stone Hen, he usually abandons the walking device to run, swing, and jump more freely. Another child, who rarely uses any spoken language at the public school, uses two- and three-word sentences at Stone Hen.

Laura attributes the children's growth to the wonders of nature and children's receptiveness to it. "Nature doesn't exclude or place restrictions on children. Children, more so than adults, are openly receptive and naturally drawn to the wonders of nature. This is true for all children despite any special needs they may have. Nature connects us all regardless of any label or demographic, reminding us of the global citizenship to which we all belong."

*Based on personal correspondence with Laura Brothwell

program. The website Kids Gardening (https://kidsgardening.org/) offers garden-based activities and lesson plans.

Dunst (2020) calls attention to the importance of identifying and attending to child interests and considering how interesting an activity is to a child. Dunst provides an example of how a walk on a nature trail can offer many informal learning opportunities. For example, a child may discover small animals, flowers, and berries. These affordances evoke engagement with the environment, such as observing, touching, and tasting. An accompanying adult can support a child's learning in this situation by showing interest in what the child finds interesting. Together, they can share the experience of interacting, and later they can learn more about what they have experienced.

Sheila Williams Ridge, author of *Nature-Based Learning for Young Children*, shares how she recognized a child's interest in her camera and how that supported that child's learning.

> On a beautiful fall day, I brought my digital camera to work to use in the classroom. All of the children enjoyed learning how to use the camera and took pictures of everything from trees to shoes. One child in particular, Clarissa, was drawn to the technology and showed joy and excitement in using this new tool. She has several developmental delays and some speech impairments but was able to effectively communicate that she wanted a few turns with the camera. When it was her turn, she took insightful photos of peers and nature. Her photos differed from the others in their composition. She would take a photo of something from far away, then move a little closer, and with each photo she would get closer to the object. She focused on photos of children in the classroom engaged in play and, by the last photo, would be taking a photo focused on the child's face. Her slow and steady approach and study of the subjects demonstrated a real focus. One of her sets of thirteen photos started from across the playground and it was hard to make out what she was taking a photo of, but every step closer the participants and their activity became clear: she was interested in the children and a school volunteer who were painting. After that set, she handed me the camera, and joined in their play.
>
> Offering children a tool to explore their environment, find an area of focus, and then pursue and study it further, or just join in the play, is a great way to utilize cameras in the classroom.

SUCCESSFUL INCLUSION IN NATURAL ENVIRONMENTS

Many early childhood education programs today are inclusive, meaning that children with special needs are included in the regular classroom. But inclusion means far more than physical access or physical presence; true inclusion includes instructional and social integration as well. At one time, instruction at different skill levels consisted of the teacher choosing a topic and then developing different lessons and activities with different objectives for each skill level. With students grouped according to skill level, the teacher moved from group to group, providing assistance as needed. An alternative to this approach is to plan lessons and activities that allow for differing levels of participation. This more inclusive approach allows all the students to participate in the same activity but at their own skill level.

So how can children who have special needs participate successfully in nature-based learning? Professionals working in the field of early childhood education are familiar with developmentally appropriate practices (DAP) as a framework for promoting young children's optimal learning and development. Children's development by age is an important part of DAP, but an understanding of the variations of each individual child—culture, strengths, interests, and needs—is also necessary. At times, approaches to early intervention for children with disabilities tend to focus more on needs—especially in relation to areas of disability—than on the strengths and interests of the child. Instead, consider the whole child in the planning what is in the best interests of a child.

Early childhood special-education professionals might use the term *exceptionality-appropriate practices* in reference to adaptations for children with disabilities. Adaptations can be made to schedules, materials and/or equipment, the social and physical environment, the level of adult support, and in what is expected from the child. Consider the following examples of ways to adapt the classroom and teaching practices for children with special needs so teachers can focus on children's strengths and interests:

✿ For children with social, emotional, and behavioral challenges:
- Provide extra structure for activities and use of materials, such as a defined physical space for activities and boundaries for use of materials, such as a tray for manipulating loose parts.
- Allow reluctant children to observe group activities until they are ready to participate.
- Schedule calming activities after vigorous play.
- Provide extra support during transition times.
- Maintain a consistent routine.

✿ For children with hearing impairments:
- Provide visual clues, such as pictures and gestures.
- Combine demonstrations with verbal instructions.
- Stay in the child's visual field.
- Be mindful of the fact that hearing aids not only amplify wanted sounds, such as speech information, but also environmental noise.

✿ For children with visual impairments:
- Provide more tactile and auditory experiences.
- Use hand-over-hand guidance when necessary.
- Place materials at the child's level.
- Provide boundaries, such as trays, boxes, and baskets, for loose materials.

✿ For children with sensory and/or anxiety issues:
- Bring a bucket of snow indoors, if playing with snow outdoors seems overwhelming.
- Keep animals in an enclosed structure, such as a tank or cage for fish, birds, or turtles, for observation.
- Watch for signs of discomfort, especially in cold, hot, or rainy weather.

✿ For children with motor difficulties:

- Provide sufficient space for maneuvering a wheelchair and other special equipment.
- Provide elevated working areas.
- Use bolsters for floor activities.
- Provide adaptive seating, as needed.
- Allow extra time for completing tasks.
- Provide larger wheels on walkers and wheelchairs for navigating sand, grass, and other bumpy or soft terrain.
- Always ask a child before providing assistance.

✿ For children with developmental delays:

- Keep directions and explanations simple, organized, and sequenced.
- Break down tasks and other activities into simple steps.

But how much adapting is too much? While adaptations can increase a child's chance of success in particular situations, they can also lead to unintended consequences. For example, making adaptations when a child could figure things out on his own can lead to a form of learned helplessness that may hinder the child from becoming more independent and developing a sense of self-efficacy. It's important for children to discover ways in which they can exercise some control over situations and environments. Once children learn this, they will be more likely to interact with the environment and with others with greater zest and joy. For children to be independent and to develop feelings of competence and self-esteem, they need to encounter the world as it is and develop strategies, whenever possible, for solving the problems they encounter.

The extent and type of support and/or adaptation should always be made on an individual basis. Several questions may be helpful in deciding when modifications should be made:

✿ Is this adaptation necessary?

✿ Is this adaptation the least intrusive way to help the child?

✿ Does this adaptation preserve the dignity of the child?

✿ Have the interests, wishes, and ideas of the child been considered in deciding whether or not—and in what way—to modify the environment?

✿ What does this adaptation say to the child? Does it say, "You are not able"?

Adults working with young children with special needs need to be aware of not only the physical barriers the children may face in interacting with their environment but also the more subtle barriers that exist in certain language and social conventions that suggest to the children that they are incompetent. The success of an intervention program or an approach in working with young children with special needs should be evaluated not by how many adaptations are made, but by how independent the children become, how competent they feel, and to what extent they experience a rich quality of life.

Patti Bailie, Associate Professor of Early Childhood Education at the University of Maine at Farmington, describes here how she learned how to be more inclusive for children with special needs.

Hiking in natural environments—a common practice for many nature-based preschools—can be challenging for children with differing physical abilities. Staff at the Schlitz Audubon Nature Center Preschool were thus hesitant to enroll a child with special needs when we were approached by the child's parents. We wondered how we could accommodate her during the daily hikes in various natural habitats. The child was four years old and had physical developmental delays. She was smaller than the other children her age and had some difficulty walking confidently. She attended a special education class three days a week. Against the advice of her doctor, who felt the program would be too challenging for her, her parents requested enrollment in the preschool.

I was the director of the nature preschool at the time and met with the child's special-education teachers for advice on how to help the child develop her physical abilities. Together, we developed a step-by-step plan. Initially, a teacher would hold the child's hand when walking on the trails, especially on uneven ground. For the next step, the child would walk on her own beside a teacher, allowing her to get assistance if needed. Over time, the child was able to walk alone and keep up with the other children. She also spent time in the natural play area shoveling wood chips and pushing wheelbarrows.

I met the parents several years later, when the child was in the sixth grade. The parents reported that their child's physical development was now on par with her peers, and they credited the nature preschool experience for playing an important role in making this happen.

The Importance of Risk Taking

Risk taking is a part of the process of developing autonomy, and all children should have opportunities to take manageable risks. Risk taking helps children earn self-respect and the respect of others. Through taking risks, children learn to assume greater responsibility for what occurs in their daily lives and can be equipped to assume responsibilities that are expected later in life. Shielding children with special needs from taking manageable risks interferes with their right to make choices and to exert control in their everyday lives.

Unfortunately, assumptions about limited capabilities tend to complicate and structure the everyday experiences of many children with special needs. There's a tendency to locate risks within the child with special needs rather than within the activity. This approach emphasizes children's deficits rather than their assets. At times, the adult response is to provide one-to-one support and supervision. Communities sometimes respond by banning children's use of certain public spaces. Well-meaning adults may say, for example, "Do not climb the trees," or "Do not climb on rocks,"

PROGRAM SPOTLIGHT
FOREST DAY LEARNING FOR YOUNG CHILDREN WHO ARE DEAF

The New Mexico School for the Deaf (NMSD) in Santa Fe was founded more than 100 years ago. Today, NMSD students attend school in multiple sites throughout the state of New Mexico, including a forest setting in the Sangre de Cristo Mountains and in the Tijeras Canyon. The students visit these outdoor classrooms bimonthly for a special experience called the Forest Day Learning (FDL) program. NMSD is the first school for the Deaf in the United States, and very possibly the first in the world, to offer a forest-school component.

The Forest Day Learning program was initiated by Sally Anderson, who was the administrator of the NMSD Albuquerque preschool at the time. After reading Richard Louv's book *Last Child in the Woods*, Sally started taking students on regular visits to a local nature center. Unfortunately, nature center rules prohibited the children from climbing trees, throwing stones in the river, building forts, and truly engaging with and in this natural setting in a completely child-led way. Sally, therefore, looked to the forest school pedagogy as an alternative. She became a licensed forest school practitioner, convinced the NMSD administrators of the benefits of forest school for young children, and launched the Forest Day Learning (FDL) program in 2016.

Children begin preparing for the FDL program at eighteen months old through regular visits to wooded parks that have no manufactured play equipment. At the age of three, children "graduate" to regular visits in the forest. Each preschool and kindergarten class enjoys FDL once every two to three weeks; each class makes at least ten visits to the same site throughout the school year.

One of the biggest challenges the teachers and therapists faced at the launch of the FDL program was the need to deprogram the children from their highly scheduled, highly structured, and risk-adverse lives. The children typically have to learn how to engage with the forest and how to play freely, as most have not had these experiences early on in their lives.

Many of the children in this program have significant language delays, even in American Sign Language (ASL), so the teachers

continued on page 27

or "I'll hold your hand as you walk across the stones." Such protectionist strategies curtail children's risk-taking opportunities. Researchers studying this phenomenon, such as Grace Spencer and colleagues (2015), call for trust and letting go as children engage in healthy risk-taking. See chapter 8 for a discussion about teachers intentionally stepping back from their role as active supervisors and encouraging more independence and risk taking for children with special needs.

Children with special needs tend to seek and enjoy the same nature-related experiences as other children. They enjoy being near animals, playing in and with water, harvesting berries, digging in the dirt, and taking risks. Their access to natural areas and opportunities to interact with natural materials may, however, be more limited due to physical disabilities and/or physical or social barriers in the environment. Social barriers, in some cases, reflect a tendency to overprotect.

Charlotte Bates (2020), a sociologist with Cardiff University, worked with the children and staff at a school in envisioning a new future for their outdoor environment. This school served children from disadvantaged backgrounds as well as children with special needs. What evolved over time was a master plan that included an outdoor classroom, various gardens, a woodland play area, a wildflower maze, an amphitheater, a fire pit, an orchard path, a zip wire, a beehive, and a chicken run. The plan included connections between all of the different areas, so that children would have access to the entire site. While feedback from the school staff indicated that this design challenged their attitudes about surveillance and risk, the plan went forward.

Dr. Bates returned about a year later after most of the changes had been implemented, and she asked the children to take pictures and write captions of their favorite places in the transformed schoolyard.

continued from page 26

and therapists created a number of visual and learning supports to assist the children in playing and exploring safely in the forest. These supports include neon cording to mark the forest classroom perimeter, brightly colored vests so that the children can be seen at all times, different colored vest for adults so that they can be found at all times, and visual cue cards meant to guide the children in safety.

One cue card features a picture of two children climbing and the number 2; it means that two children can climb at a time. Teachers can tack this cue card to a favorite climbing tree. Other visual cues include picture exchange communication system (PECS) cards to use with children who have had an additional diagnosis of autism and/or with children who are not yet communicating in ASL. At times, teachers use a visual schedule depicting the choices available and the schedule for the FDL day. Additionally, the teachers spend lots of time preteaching and front-loading important information, such as why it is important to stay within the forest classroom boundary, what animals they may come across, and how they dress for the forest and why. They practice "gathering drills" to keep everyone safe. The adults even made a video for the children demonstrating how to move hands and feet from one branch to another for tree climbing.

The FDL program has proven to be remarkably successful. Documented outcomes include increased skill in communicating, including using ASL, and improved inquiry skills, motor skills, social-play competence, and self-confidence. Many of these skills relate directly to children's individual IEP goals. Families now see their children as being more competent and capable. Perhaps most importantly, both the children and adults show a palpable sense of wonder, awe, and joy.

Children captured pictures and wrote captions about places to hide, places to feel calm, and places with animals. Feedback from the teachers suggested that after changes were made to the outdoor play space, children started using the space in more creative ways. Teachers' behaviors changed, as well, in that they started giving the children more freedom to explore. Dr. Bates noted that, as the outdoor landscape changed and as children responded to these changes, the school's culture shifted from a culture of protection to a culture of resilience.

MOTIVATORS, BARRIERS, AND ENABLERS

Julia Sterman and colleagues (2016) investigated motivators (reasons for participating in outdoor activities), barriers (reasons for not participating), and enablers (factors that encourage participation) that children with disabilities and their families have experienced in engaging in outdoor activities. They found that caregivers, families, schools, and communities juggle many factors when making decisions about when, where, how, and if outdoor play occurs for children with disabilities.

Motivators:
- Increased overall development
- Opportunities to build self-determination
- Opportunities for fun, enjoyment, and time to be a child
- Strengthening the family unit
- Increased inclusion by peers
- Greater acceptance of children with disabilities by peers and society at large

Barriers:
- Fear of disapproval and/or exclusion by other children
- Staff's lack of knowledge about and insensitivity toward children with disabilities
- Children's health condition
- Children's skills and perception of skills, such as the ability to accurately judge safety, navigate the environment, manipulate materials, communicate wants and needs, interact positively with others, attend to an activity, understand the concepts within a play sequence, and regulate emotions
- Mobility concerns about certain physical structures, such as steps, rough terrain, and small enclosed spaces
- For some children with autism, crowded conditions and loud noises

Enablers:
- Caregivers' appreciation of the value of outdoor play
- Caregivers' awareness of opportunities for outdoor play
- Social acceptance
- Built environments that accommodate children with special needs
- Children's health, skills, and interests
- Time and money available for outdoor play in appropriate environments

Even though young children with special needs may benefit in multiple ways from nature-focused activities, their opportunities for participating in such activities tend to be more limited than they are for other children. While the number of forest schools and nature-based preschools is rapidly growing, few serve children with special needs. Hopefully, greater understanding of the why and how of including children with special needs in nature-related activities will lead to more inclusive practices.

Of course, including children with special needs in a forest school or nature-based preschool can be challenging. However, knowing that children with special needs are the ones who may benefit the most from such programs should motivate all of us to make the effort. Tapping into resources in the community, seeking professional development opportunities for staff, and looking to families as partners in the process can be helpful.

Anne Ouwerkerk, an early childhood special-education teacher, is a strong advocate for inclusive outdoor education. Her passion for making nature accessible for all children is nurtured by the many positive results she's witnessed during outdoor explorations. In the following vignette, Anne shares the story of how explorations in a wooded area helped one child with special needs gain the confidence and social skills he needed to initiate playful interactions with peers.

I am a preschool special education teacher. While living in New Hampshire, I was fortunate to have the opportunity and support to explore nature around our preschool. My class of students, with and without special needs, spent as much time as possible learning about and in our natural environment. We explored, had adventures, connected with each other, and studied the ever-changing world outside the concrete walls of our building. It was outside where I witnessed the greatest growth and development of the students. One student in particular stands out.

When Chase started at our preschool, he had delays in all areas of development including social, communication, play, and motor skills—delays that had been attributed to lead poisoning. According to the Centers for Disease Control and Prevention (2020), lead poisoning can damage the brain and nervous system and can cause learning and speech problems. Chase also had pediatric hydrocephalus, a condition that can cause additional delays in development. Chase tended to engage in solitary play. His imaginary play skills were limited, and he was often not attending to the world around him.

Many of my students have not had extensive outdoor experiences beyond backyards and playgrounds. I start each year by scaffolding outdoor experiences. We begin by playing on the playground, where we observe the natural world around us and learn to play safely with others. I bring natural materials into the classroom for projects, decor, and study. Eventually, our group of preschoolers is able to play in the nearby field with slightly larger boundaries. From there, we move into the woods beyond the playground and field. With each step,

TAKE ACTIVITIES OUTDOORS

One of the recommended practices for nature-based learning is to regularly conduct what are traditionally "indoor" activities, such as reading and art, outdoors. This practice rejects any notion that learning is primarily an indoor activity while play is more of an outdoor activity. It reflects the research-based understanding that play and learning are deeply connected and can occur in both indoor and outdoor environments.

An advantage of conducting reading and art activities outdoors is the way in which this can contribute to children's environmental awareness and appreciation. For example, reading about a tree or drawing a picture of a tree while indoors is far less meaningful and motivating than conducting these same activities while in the presence of real trees outside. Additionally, some children with attention or focus problems function better in an outdoor environment than they do indoors (Guardino et al., 2019).

Find more recommended practices for inclusive outdoor activities in the *Nature-Based Preschool Professional Practice Guidebook* (2019) developed by the Natural Start Alliance and *Early Childhood Environmental Education Programs: Guidelines for Excellence* (2016) developed by the North American Association for Environmental Education.

students are introduced to safety expectations, larger boundaries, and an increased awareness of their natural environment. They also gain experience navigating different terrains. Finally, we all explore the larger area beyond the playground and field, an area that includes a woods.

I worked with Chase over a period of two years. During that time, I saw improvements in his play and motor skills, verbal communication, and attention when we were outside. In earlier days, Chase would sit down and refuse to walk after short periods in the woods. During his last months at the preschool, Chase was leading walks on the trails and navigating the natural playground of the forest. His communication skills grew as he worked on building huts with peers, asked for help to move large branches, pointed out new treasures, and played games in the woods. He was fascinated and intrigued by what he experienced in the natural world around him. It was a privilege to witness the joy and confidence Chase experienced during our adventures in the forest.

For one of our adventures, we used branches to build a hut in the woods. The children created a seating area, a pretend fire pit, and even a bridge over a small stream. I clearly remember Chase sitting by the little stream and motioning to a peer to come and sit with him. Chase handed a stick to the peer, and together they pretended to fish. Chase was once a child who had limited play skills and rarely initiated conversation; yet, there he was reeling in a pretend fish with his buddy.

While every child is unique, all children share certain characteristics and certain needs. One such need is the need to be accepted and to belong. This chapter discussed ways in which nature engagement and nature-rich environments can help children with differing abilities feel that they belong. The next chapter focuses specifically on children with autism and discusses ways in which nature-rich environments and activities can not only address their unique needs but also can nurture their special capabilities and strengths.

REFERENCES

Barfield, Patricia A. and Martha Driessnack. 2018. "Children with ADHD Draw-and-Tell about What Makes Their Life Really Good." *Journal for Specialists in Pediatric Nursing* 23(2): e12210.

Bates, Charlotte. 2020. "Rewilding Education? Exploring an Imagined and Experienced Outdoor Learning Space." *Children's Geographies* 18(3): 364–374.

Centers for Disease Control and Prevention. 2020. "Health Effects of Lead Exposure." Centers for Disease Control and Prevention. https://www.cdc.gov/nceh/lead/prevention/health-effects.htm

Di Carmine, Francesca, and Rita Berto. 2020. "Contact with Nature Can Help ADHD Children to Cope with Their Symptoms: The State of the Evidence and Future Directions for Research." *Visions for Sustainability.* doi: https://doi.org/10.13135/2384-8677/4883

Dunst, Carl J. 2000. "Revisiting 'Rethinking Early Intervention.'" *Topics in Early Childhood Special Education* 20(2): 95–103.

Grandin, Temple. 2020. *Different, Not Less.* Arlington, TX: Future Horizons.

Guardino, Caroline, et al. 2019. "Teacher and Student Perceptions of an Outdoor Classroom." *Journal of Outdoor and Environmental Education* 22(2): 113–126.

Spencer, Grace, et al. 2016. "Uncertainty in the School Playground: Shifting Rationalities and Teachers' Sense-Making in the Management of Risks for Children with Disabilities." *Health, Risk and Society* 18(5–6): 301–317.

Sterman, Julia, et al. 2016. "Outdoor Play Decisions by Caregivers of Children with Disabilities: A Systematic Review of Qualitative Studies." *Journal of Developmental and Physical Disabilities* 28(6): 931–957.

Sterman, Julia, et al. 2020. "Creating Play Opportunities on the School Playground: Educator Experiences of the Sydney Playground Project." *Australian Occupational Therapy Journal* 67(1): 62–73.

Tiplady, Lucy S. E., and Harriet Menter. 2020. "Forest School for Wellbeing: An Environment in which Young People Can 'Take What They Need.'" *Journal of Adventure Education and Outdoor Learning* 21(2): 99–114.

CHAPTER 3

Nature and Children with Autism

"

There are a thousand ways to kneel
and kiss the earth.

— JALAL AD-DIN MOHAMMAD RUMI,
Persian poet and theologian

Biodiversity—or biological diversity—is a familiar concept referring to the wide variety of animals and plants in the ecosystems around us. Generally, greater diversity of life within an ecosystem reflects a stronger and more resilient ecosystem that is better equipped to sustain itself when faced with external stresses. Consider, for example, how plant and animal species in a lake depend upon each other for food. Small fish often depend on aquatic plants; larger fish depend on the smaller fish. If the lake has just one type of aquatic plant and the entire species dies, small fish will die, too. In turn, larger fish will die. This sets the stage for ecosystem collapse. If the lake includes different types of aquatic plants and different types of small fish, the loss of one type of plant or fish will not have the same devastating effect. Healthy ecosystems tend to have different parts doing essential jobs. Different types of aquatic plants feeding the small fish will help keep the lake healthy. Diversity in an ecosystem, then, is a strength, as it makes important contributions to the overall health of the ecosystem.

Neurodiversity—perhaps a less familiar concept—refers to the variations in the ways human brains function, our *neurocognition*. Biodiversity is the key to healthy ecosystems; it's a necessity for life to flourish. Diversity in the human population is the key to a healthy human society. Evolution favors diversity. Yet, we tend to place greater value on what we refer to as "typical."

Just a few decades ago, the terms *autism* and *autism spectrum disorder* (ASD) weren't a part of everyday language, nor were they included in a listing of different types of disabilities. Today, almost everyone has heard of autism and is aware of the rapid increase in the number of children diagnosed with autism. This awareness, however, doesn't always lead to understanding and acceptance. Children with autism/ASD are unique individuals and have various kinds of needs. What they want includes acceptance and opportunities to develop their capabilities. While chapter 2 discussed how nature can help promote the development of children with disabilities, this chapter focuses specifically on the unique characteristics of children with ASD and discusses ways in which nature engagement can promote their holistic development.

※

Defining Autism

We use the term *neurotypical* in reference to a style of neurocognitive functioning that is viewed as "normal" within dominant social standards. Autism is a form of *neurodivergence*—diversity in neurocognition. Unfortunately, discussions about ASD often highlight deficiencies and a search for interventions to minimize the deficiencies. Some researchers and practitioners, however, advocate a different approach. They call for replacing the deficiency-oriented framework with new thinking and new terminology focusing on the strengths of individuals with ASD (Armstrong, 2017; Masataka, 2017). Consistent with this new thinking is the idea of referring to persons with ASD as being *neurodiverse* instead of "deficient." Instead of trying to "fix the problem," efforts focus on creating supportive environments where persons with ASD are respected and nurtured for their capabilities and strengths. This approach is based on the understanding that neurodiversity is something we should recognize and celebrate.

The term *autism spectrum disorder* was introduced a number of years ago to add more understanding about what was generally referred to as autism. While this change in terminology was meant to clarify some issues, it remains troublesome for a number of reasons. For many people, the term *autism spectrum disorder* is hard to understand; for some, it specifies a disorder versus a condition. Perhaps the term *autism spectrum condition* (ASC) would be a more acceptable term.

We know that people with autism face many daily living challenges differently than people who do not have autism. These challenges generally relate to social communication and/or interaction and a tendency to engage in restricted and/or repetitive behaviors. Yet, each person with autism is a unique individual and has a unique way of viewing and relating to the world.

People with autism are sometimes described as "being on the spectrum." This term avoids the "disorder" label, while still referencing some form or degree of autism. It recognizes the fact that people with autism have characteristics that fall into a range, from relatively mild to very severe. Differences in IQ account for a great deal of this variability. Temperament, interests, and unique skill patterns also make a difference.

Autism is a neurodevelopmental condition that affects the way the brain performs in areas of communication skills and social interaction. Many people with ASD find it difficult to initiate and/or sustain a conversation. They may avoid eye contact and display unusual facial expressions. They may become intensely absorbed in a particular object, repeating motor movements over and over, and engaging in nonfunctional routines such as insisting on eating only foods of a certain color (Willis, 2006; Mesibov, Shea, and Schopler, 2004). These behaviors may interfere with quality of life.

Quality of Life for Children with Autism

The concept of neurodiversity can shed light on efforts to improve the quality of life for children with autism. Neurodiversity calls attention to the strengths and gifts versus the "disabilities" of people with ASD. Such gifts often include enhanced auditory and visual discrimination capabilities. Hyper-sensation and hyper-attention to detail are highly adaptive for living in nature, suggesting that during prehistoric times these abilities may have had an evolutionary advantage (Armstrong, 2017). In other words, some of the characteristics of ASD aren't errors or mistakes of nature, but are instead invaluable aspects of human genetic variability (Masataka, 2017).

People with ASD may seem disabled because their gifts are not in sync with modern civilization. Exposure to nature, then, can relieve the concerns and improve quality of life for people with autism. While everyone can benefit from engagement with nature, the benefits of such engagement may be greater for individuals with ASD, including the following:

- ✿ Improved communication
- ✿ More positive social interactions
- ✿ Increased physical activity
- ✿ Cognitive development
- ✿ Greater expressions of emotions (Barakat, Bakr, and El-Sayad, 2019)

Some studies even refer to the nature benefits for people with ASD as "nature as a healer" (Barakat, Bakr, and El-Sayad, 2019) and "the healing balm of nature" (Armstrong, 2017). Nature, then, in addition to the other benefits it offers, can be a source of solace for people with ASD.

In their 2020 article in *Psychology Today*, "5 Messages for My Younger Autistic Self: Things We Wish We Had Known While Growing Up Undiagnosed with Autism," authors Erin Bulluss and Abby Sesterka suggest that seeing, being, and doing things differently can be "a beautiful thing." The authors describe how a person with autism may see details that others miss, make connections that others can't fathom, and experience intensity in ways that only an autistic mind is able to do. They conclude by noting that people with autism "are not broken, or damaged, or wrong." They are, instead, "superbly, supremely, splendidly autistic."

Sensory-Processing Issues and Nature-Based Interventions

While social interaction issues tend to be a major challenge for many children with special needs, sensory-processing problems are common, especially for children on the autism spectrum. Children with ASD may exhibit behaviors such as the following:

- ✿ Self-stimulating, such as hand flapping and excessive rocking
- ✿ Avoidance, such as covering one's ears to block noises
- ✿ Sensory seeking, such as twirling and licking
- ✿ Tuning out, such as not responding when their name is called

Sensory-related problem behaviors may also show up as difficulty with completing a purposeful plan of action (Willis, 2006).

Sensory processing is the ability to receive and understand sensory data from the environment and from one's own body. An individual with sensory-processing dysfunction may not be able to regulate or filter out the information (the *stimuli*) he or she receives from the senses and thus has trouble adapting to the everyday sensations that most people take for granted. While many children with autism exhibit sensory-processing dysfunction, the way they react to stimuli varies. Some have *hyper* (elevated) sensitivity with intense responses to stimuli such as light or sounds. Others have *hypo* (underresponsive) sensitivity to sensory input, as in a lack of awareness of extreme heat or cold. People with autism who are hypersensitive may engage in self-stimulatory behaviors, such as head banging or rocking, to suppress pain or calm themselves down. People with autism who are hyposensitive may seek sensory stimulation from their environment, such as by twirling, making loud noises, bumping into others, or chewing on non-food items (Willis, 2006).

Children with sensory-processing problems may have trouble knowing where their body is in space. They may thus be more at risk for physical injuries, more inclined to invade other people's space, and more likely to have difficulty with gross- and fine-motor activities. They may also engage in antisocial and violent behaviors. At times, they may withdraw or refuse to participate in an activity (Willis, 2006; Mesibov, Shea, and Schopler, 2004). It's not unusual for families of children with ASD to limit participation in social and community activities due to concerns about their child's sensory-processing problems and related behaviors.

Lots of movement and a variety of sensory-rich experiences can generally help children with sensory-processing problems. The outdoors is an excellent

RESEARCH NOTE:
BENEFITS OF OUTDOOR EXPERIENCES FOR CHILDREN WITH AUTISM

In one study, researchers interviewed twenty-two families of children with ASD about their children's experience in natural environments (Li et al., 2018). All of the families identified numerous benefits for their children associated with time in nature, including positive sensorimotor, emotional, and social outcomes. The most frequently mentioned benefit was positive affect or happiness. Families reported that while their children were outdoors, they seemed especially attracted to loose elements such as sand, water, leaves, and twigs, which held their children's attention for an extended period. Almost all the families felt that the interactions with these materials enhanced their children's gross- and fine-motor skills. They also noted how the natural environment tended to have a calming effect on their children. The families described ways in which their children seemed happy, energetic, and lively in nature.

In another study, researchers investigated the effect of an outdoor adventure program on children between the ages of three and seven with ASD in a special education program (Zachor et al., 2017). The children were divided into two groups. Some participated in challenging physical activities requiring cooperation and communication with peers and instructors; others participated in a classroom-only program. In addition to increasing awareness of the environment, the outdoor adventure program promoted personal and social development using all the senses. The researchers found that the outdoor adventure program had a significant effect on ASD symptom severity. Children who participated in the outdoor program showed a greater reduction in ASD symptoms and impressive gains in verbal and nonverbal communication, imitation, and social reciprocal behavior than children not participating in the outdoor program. Over the same period, children participating in the classroom-only program showed an increase in the severity of restricted and repetitive behaviors. These behavioral concerns were not noted in the children participating in the outdoor adventure program.

setting for gross- and fine-motor activities—running, jumping, climbing, digging, stacking, picking, building, and so on. The outdoors is also an excellent setting for enjoying sensory-rich experiences through touch, sight, sound, taste, and smell. Angela Hanscom, a pediatric occupational therapist, writes about the importance of outdoor play for promoting children's confidence, strength, and competence. In her book *Balanced and Barefoot*, Hanscom (2016) also discusses the role of outdoor play in promoting sensory integration. She says that the more sensory experiences a child has throughout the day, the more integrated and organized the brain, senses, and body become. According to Hanscom, the outdoors offers a perfectly balanced sensory experience.

Many sensory experiences in the out-of-doors can be calming for children with ASD and may contribute to self-regulation. For children who are hypersensitive, cave-like places—such as a secluded spot under low-hanging branches—can help a child regroup when feeling stressed or on sensory overload. The dappled shade of a forest environment can provide coolness and soften harsh sunlight. The smell, touch, sound—and in some cases, taste—of the natural environment can help with sensory-processing issues. Many wild plants are naturally fragrant, and their leaves and stems come in a variety of textures, shapes, colors, and sizes. Bark, grass, pebbles, sand, soil, and water offer textures that can be stimulating for a child with ASD. Listening to the wind in the trees, birdsong, running water, and the buzz of insects can also be stimulating and help with sensory processing.

Physical Activity and the Outdoor Environment

Muscle tone, balance, and physical strength tend to be lower in children with ASD (Willis, 2006). Physical activity in a natural environment can contribute to stronger muscles and more developed gross- and fine-motor skills. An increase in physical skills often leads to an increase in confidence, self-esteem, and social acceptance.

Many children with autism also have difficulty with knowing where their body is in space. They may bump into furniture and to other people. This may be due to an underdeveloped proprioceptive sense—the sense that receives information from joints, muscles, and ligaments (Willis, 2006). Tree climbing and some other outdoor physical activities can be excellent ways to promote the proprioceptive sense.

It's natural for young children to be physically active. They're prone to run, climb, reach, and throw. Peers often serve as a motivator for increased physical activity. Motor and social-interaction challenges, however, can place children with ASD at risk for limited physical activity. A child with ASD may want to join a group of children in running and climbing but not know how to join or have the necessary motor skills to actively participate. The child may thus become an onlooker or engage in such maladaptive or stereotypic and less physically active behaviors such as body rocking.

While stereotypic behaviors, such as body rocking, may help a child with ASD cope with stressful situations, they can also create social stigma and reduce the number of opportunities for positive social interactions. Substituting more active and healthier forms of physical activity for stereotypic behaviors offers numerous benefits for children with ASD, including enhancing their social status, promoting social inclusion, reducing stress, and maintaining a healthier weight (Lang et al., 2010).

One way to promote physical activity is to provide an environment that invites such activity. A child with ASD may find a natural environment more inviting than a traditional playground. Forests come equipped with stumps, logs, and fallen trees, and natural environments may feature rocks, vines, and hiking trails, all of which are open ended and invite different types of movement. Nature can be a welcome alternative to settings and situations where behaviors are more prescribed. The open-endedness gives children more freedom to be themselves, to follow their interests, and to test their own limits.

Supportive Environments for Children with Autism

Both nature and nurture play a role in how humans grow and develop. *Nature*, in this sense, refers to all the genes and hereditary factors that contribute to a person's unique physical appearance, personality, and physiology. *Nurture* is defined as the environmental factors that affect a person, such as childhood experiences, family and social relationships, culture, community, and physical environment. Neurodiversity in the human population suggests that not everyone will respond in the same way to the nurture-related influences in our lives. We do know that nature and nurture are interdependent, working dynamically together in child development.

Children with ASD may benefit differently and in more dramatic ways from engagement with the natural environment than other children. In fact, the most supportive environment for children with ASD could be ones offering rich opportunities for deep engagement with nature, such as forest schools, care farms, and sensory gardens.

FOREST SCHOOLS

Participating in a forest school program is one way to give a child with autism rich opportunities for nature engagement. A typical forest-school session is several hours long with the entire session being held outdoors. While each session is planned and led by a trained forest school practitioner, the activities are child centered and child led. Learners have the time and space to develop their own interests, skills, and understandings through practical, hands-on experiences. A hallmark of the forest-school experience is the freedom to explore, play, build, imagine, take risks, and use one's senses to experience the natural environment and to engage with one another.

While forest school supports the development of a positive lifelong relationship between the child and the natural world, it also supports the development of the whole child. The connections children make during forest school are with themselves, other children, the forest school practitioner (teacher), and the forest itself. The forest provides the kind of physical space that matches well the needs and interests of each individual child, including a child with ASD. While the forest is a sensory-rich environment, it also provides quiet spaces with minimal demands or expectations. Just as the trees and other plants in the forest grow at their own pace and in their own way, so do children as they play and explore in this environment. Social interactions aren't forced; they unfold at each child's own pace.

The forest works in partnership with the teachers and therapists, in that it provides a meaningful and positive environment for promoting intervention goals in all the different domains of child development. Observing children interacting with the elements of the forest allows the adults to deepen their understanding about each individual child—her sensory needs, special interests, abilities, and communication needs. For the individual child, the forest offers unending opportunities for pursuing individual interests, testing individual limits, and engaging in ongoing explorations. Children are free to join in with a group activity or spend some time in their own solitary activities.

For more information about forest schools and children with autism, I recommend *Nature Preschools and Forest Kindergartens* edited by David Sobel, *Forest School and Outdoor Learning in the Early Years* by Sara Knight, and *Nature Kindergartens and Forest Schools* by Claire Warden.

CARE FARMS

Care farming is a growing movement in countries around the world that combines agricultural production with health, social, and educational services. Care farms are working farms that welcome people to come and heal and/or learn by participating in farm activities in whatever way they can. These farms are based on the understanding that being included in farm activities is a meaningful way for people to reconnect to nature, animals, themselves, and others. Often, participants experience a sense of achievement, fulfillment, and belonging.

Care farming can involve different types of farm activities: horticulture, forestry, animal care, conservation, and woodwork. Many tasks involve teamwork and encourage meaningful interaction. Animal care, in particular, tends to reduce children's feelings of anxiety and can act as a mediator to improve social interactions with other humans. Children often find comfort in their interactions with animals and have opportunities to develop bonds and show affection.

Care farming falls within a broader framework of nature-based interventions, collectively called *green care*, that use plants, animals, and landscapes to create opportunities for improved health and well-being. Healing elements of the farm environment include its peacefulness and wide-open spaces. Being immersed in the farm's natural environment can reduce anxiety and offer a sense of "safe containment." The experience of daily and seasonal rhythms and patterns observed in nature seem to reduce the fear of change and promote the psychological development of children with autism (Byström, Grahn, and Hägerhäll, 2019).

One study conducted by researchers in the Netherlands (Ferwerda-van Zonnevelda, Oosting, and Kijlstra, 2012) focused on care farms serving children with autism. Farmers interviewed for the study noted how animals provide social support for the children, helping them gain trust and overcome fear. They described how some children tell animals complete stories and how children who feel insecure will cuddle with animals and get energy to deal with things that may be bothering them. The farmers described ways children looked to animals for moments of rest and how they became relaxed when with the animals. The researchers found that the care farms can

PROGRAM SPOTLIGHT
THE CARE FARM, LLC*

The Care Farm started with a simple idea of sharing with others the joy that animals and nature bring to me. As a social worker, I have worked with clients of different ages, abilities, needs, and backgrounds. I found that each time my clients had the opportunity to interact with farm animals and the natural environment surrounding the farm, magic started to happen! They began to smile. They began to laugh. They became engaged. They showed empathy and concern. They felt important. Their confidence started to grow. The benefits were so many and so significant that it only made sense to offer the experience to even more individuals in need of support, acceptance, and encouragement.

Located in Hollis, New Hampshire, The Care Farm offers individual and group programming to youth, adults, families, and community organizations. People, animals, and the earth work together to nurture health and well-being. The Care Farm currently is home to horses, goats, rabbits, cats, chickens, a dog, and a miniature cow who is not so miniature! Some of the animals have been rescued, and all of them adore being loved and coddled.

continued on page 42

continued from page 41

Visitors feel safe expressing themselves while at the farm in the nonjudgmental, positive, and encouraging environment. They easily begin to connect and engage with both the animals, the natural world, and other participants. Through the gentle encouragement of farm staff, clients learn and practice healthy coping skills that help reduce feelings of stress, depression, and anxiety. They develop healthy social and relationship skills and build positive self-esteem.

Though the idea of spending time outdoors interacting with animals may be simple, the benefits are many. The smiles, laughter, and general sense of well-being expressed by those who visit are a true testament to the magical connection among humans, animals, and the natural world.

*Contributed by Beth Frankel, owner and operator of The Care Farm, LLC

serve as effective opportunities for families and their children with autism to have helpful short breaks, called *respite care*.

Many children with ASD can pose severe challenges to their families, who often report high levels of stress. Short-break services give children and their families the opportunity to spend time apart from each other. The respite services offered by some care farms may be for a day, evening, overnight, weekend, or longer. Care farms that seem to work the best for children with ASD are small farms that offer enough space for each child to move about without bothering others. The rhythm and peace of daily farm activities creates a safe and predictable environment for the children. Knowing that they have different places and the freedom to withdraw when needed provides a sense of peace and comfort.

Some care farms include siblings of children with ASD. This practice can make the care farm experience more comforting for everyone involved. The Farmstead School in Asheville, North Carolina, for example, combines a farm and forest experience for young children. Their early childhood program promotes foundational academic skills, social-emotional skills, and whole-child development. Learning opportunities include hands-on lessons, community time, garden work, animal care, singing, creating, playing, storytelling, mindfulness practice, and free play. A covered platform nestled in a twenty-five-acre forest serves as the "home base" for the preschool program. Much of the day, however, is spent exploring, hiking the trails, and playing in the forest.

SENSORY GARDENS

Sensory gardens are sometimes designed specifically for children with autism. Landscape architects and occupational therapists often work together in designing these spaces, taking into consideration children's sensory-processing challenges and their hypo- and hypersensitivities. Sensory gardens support children's curiosity and meaningful engagement, offer both alerting and calming sensory experiences, and can allay children's stress and anxiety while gently enriching their basic senses of sight, hearing, smell, touch, and taste. A sensory garden can also promote children's vestibular (balance) and proprioceptive (body position and movement in space) senses. Well-designed sensory gardens bring solace, excitement, engagement, and learning all in one space.

Children can play and explore in sensory gardens with greater freedom than they would have in a typical garden. The spaces are sometimes surrounded by a fence to give children greater freedom of movement and exploration while still keeping them safe. The overarching intent of the garden is to offer serenity, security, autonomy, flexibility, and restoration, allowing each child to interact in ways they need or want to.

A well-designed sensory garden invites children to feel whole and safe on their own terms. Children experience reprieve in the garden's getaway areas, such as a small chair or bench under low-hanging branches, and enrichment by exploring plants and other sensory features throughout the garden. Some sensory gardens offer areas where it's safe for children to walk barefoot, which can, in turn, sharpen the child's foot perception and sense of touch. Such areas might feature

PROGRAM SPOTLIGHT
TURN BACK TIME*

In 2002, my husband and I accepted two siblings as a foster-care placement in our home; we adopted them in 2006. We were camping with some friends when we noted how our son, who usually had difficulty connecting with others because of his autism and intellectual disability, was playing at a stream with other children. As the children were catching frogs, our son was in on the action, communicating and having less conflict than usual. We wondered whether there was a connection between nature experiences and improved language and social skills in children with autism. We discovered—with the help of Richard Louv's book, *Last Child in the Woods*—that the children did better emotionally and socially when they were outside or connecting with animals.

A few years later, we decided to start a farm for children with special needs. Turn Back Time is a fifty-eight-acre property that features a working farm, a nature playground, an active beaver pond, and an extensive trail system. We offer a summer camp that serves more than six hundred children of all abilities per year. The mission of Turn Back Time includes helping people recognize nature's ability to teach and heal. The farm is a great equalizer, because in nature children are not constrained by any diagnosis, disorder, shape, size, or age. The programming includes nature exploration, farm education, and play.

At Turn Back Time, everyone is a rock star, and staff work hard to find each child's competency. A "challenge by choice" philosophy helps each child find his or her place at the farm and allows personal growth and resiliency through experiences. We believe—and research confirms—that play and nature are essential to every child's development. It's through play and nature that children learn to navigate the world around them.

In 2013, the mother of an eight-year-old named Jake called to inquire about our program. She had heard about the farm from Jake's therapist, who had been working with the family to stabilize their home environment. Jake loved animals and being outside. As we talked, his mother became so excited about the prospect that Jake might be able to go to a place that would make him feel good about himself and help him to be successful that she began to cry.

Jake came to camp with his brother for several weeks that year. The staff worked with Jake through collaborative problem solving and

continued on page 45

grass, soft moss, clay, sand, smooth stones, and shallow water. Avoid toxic plants as well as stagnant water when developing a sensory garden.

The following list offers tips of what to include when creating a sensory garden for children with autism:

- ❀ Wide pathways and surfaces to avoid the feeling of crowding

- ❀ Non-glare surfacing materials for children with photosensitivity

- ❀ Plenty of shade provided by trees, vine-covered trellises, and shade structures

- ❀ Elements of consistency, such as stone walls and hedges and other types of vegetation, arranged in a predictable pattern

- ❀ Physical transitions between spaces to allow for a pause before entering and to be able to see the entire area

- ❀ Opportunities for socialization, such as seating arranged for small groups

- ❀ Plenty of visual aids, such as orientation maps and other types of signs

- ❀ Soothing getaway areas

- ❀ Hammocks

continued from page 44

our "challenge by choice" philosophy. This approach helped Jake find things that worked best for him on the farm. He took care of the animals, "worked" with staff on farm chores, and even became the resident expert on the farm dog! Jake was able to become a mentor to younger children in the multiage camp. This experience helped him stay emotionally regulated and assured him that he had something to contribute to the small farm community.

Although there were some moments when Jake needed support and guidance from experienced staff, his time on the farm was no different than that of his peers. All the children experienced a child-directed, play-based camp that builds resilience and autonomy through nature activities. Jake's clinician heard from Jake about his experiences and came for a visit. As she told the staff, "I just had to see what this was all about!" At the end of her visit, she noted, "Nowhere ever has [Jake] had success like this."

Jake went on to attend camp for three more years, attending multiple weeks each summer. He grew his leadership skills and became a support to staff, particularly when it came to teaching policy and procedures to children during their care time with animals. As he was leaving the farm one year after camp, Jake said, "Good-bye, pure bliss."

*Contributed by Lisa Burris, cofounder and executive director of Turn Back Time, a nonprofit farm and nature-based program in Paxton, Massachusetts

❁ Plants appealing to the five basic senses (sight, hearing, smell, touch, and taste)

❁ Planters of varying heights to bring sensory-appropriate plants to easily accessible levels

❁ Wide-open spaces and small, enclosed areas

❁ Opportunities for risk-taking, such as climbing trees or using stepping stones to cross a stream

❁ Habitats for wildlife, such as birds and butterflies

❁ Places for walking barefoot

PROGRAM SPOTLIGHT
SENSORY GARDEN AT ELS CENTER OF EXCELLENCE

The Els Center of Excellence in Jupiter, Florida, hosts a variety of programs and services for individuals with autism. Its campus includes a sensory-arts garden that serves as a therapeutic and educational destination for children and adults of all abilities. The garden was designed to offer varying levels of sensory experiences while minimizing sensory overload (Wagenfeld, Sotelo, and Kamp 2019). Individuals with autism have opportunities to engage with nature through observation and/or interaction with birds, other animals, and plants and to develop social skills. The garden includes a variety of plantings, hardscape, and water features that stimulate motor, cognitive, sensory, and social skills.

A multidisciplinary team of professionals worked together in designing the garden. While they focused on meeting the special needs of individuals with ASD, they also wanted a garden setting that would be welcoming to the larger community, including families, educators, therapists, and caretakers. By making the garden a destination for community events, it also promotes the value, acceptance, and inclusion of individuals with ASD.

Every plant, material, and furnishing of the garden was carefully chosen for its appropriateness, safety, durability, and therapeutic potential. The design strategy reflects a combination of health-promoting design principles and an understanding of the unique needs of children and youth with ASD. The garden includes a number of sensory "rooms," targeting each of the five senses. A dark band circling each room provides a subtle visual boundary and signals a change in sensory experience. The garden also features a series of "places away"—places offering reduced and integrated sensory experiences. These areas can be especially helpful for people with ASD who may experience hypersensitivity or need a moment of respite and refuge.

The garden is described as a place that "provides opportunity and choice for everyone to engage with nature on their own terms, in their own way, and at their own pace."

Challenges and Rewards
When Working with Children with Autism

Families, teachers, and other professionals face many challenges in working with children with ASD, as these children often exhibit behaviors that are hard to understand. Some behaviors need to be modified for the health and well-being of the individual child and the people around the child. It's helpful to know that nature can be a friend or collaborator in the process. It's also encouraging to know that children—including children with special needs—are naturally drawn to plants, animals, and other features of the natural world. Tapping into the gifts of nature and the biophilic tendencies of children can support the work of adults as they interact with children with ASD.

All children tend to enjoy better outcomes when their interests are supported. Nature offers an unending supply of materials and happenings to excite the interest and curiosity of almost any child. Time in nature gives children the opportunity to explore their interests and make new discoveries about themselves and the world around them. Nature can also soothe and relax a child with ASD. Nature-related experiences tend to promote a child's self-regulation, confidence, and self-esteem. In myriad ways, time in nature makes important contributions to a child's quality of life.

As discussed in this chapter, the sensory-rich and soothing aspects of nature may be especially helpful for children with ASD. Chapter 4 discusses ways in which nature as teacher can also make life richer and more meaningful for children with varying abilities.

REFERENCES

Armstrong, Thomas. 2017. "The Healing Balm of Nature: Understanding and Supporting the Naturalist Intelligence in Individuals Diagnosed with ASD: Comment on: 'Implications of the Idea of Neurodiversity for Understanding the Origins of Developmental Disorders' by Nobuo Masataka." *Physics of Life Reviews* 20: 109–111.

Barakat, Hadeer Abd-El-Razak, Ali Bakr, and Zeyad El-Sayad. 2019. "Nature as a Healer for Autistic Children." *Alexandria Engineering Journal* 58(1): 353–366.

Bulluss, Erin, and Abby Sesterka. 2020. "5 Messages for My Younger Autistic Self: Things We Wish We Had Known While Growing Up Undiagnosed with Autism." *Psychology Today* September/October: 30–31.

Byström, Kristina, Patrik Grahn, and Caroline Hägerhäll. 2019. "Vitality from Experiences in Nature and Contact with Animals—A Way to Develop Joint Attention and Social Engagement in Children with Autism?" *International Journal of Environmental Research and Public Health* 16(23): 4673

Ferwerda-van Zonnevelda, R.T., Simon Oosting, and A. Kijlstra. 2012. "Care Farms as Short-Break Service for Children with Autism Spectrum Disorders." *NJAS Wageninen Journal of Life Sciences* 59(1–2): 35–40.

Hanscom, Angela. 2016. *Balanced and Barefoot: How Unrestricted Outdoor Play Makes for Strong, Confident, and Capable Children*. Oakland, CA: New Harbinger.

Lang, Russell, et al. 2010. "Physical Exercise and Individuals with Autism Spectrum Disorders: A Systematic Review." *Research in Autism Spectrum Disorders* 4(4): 565–576.

Li, Dongying, et al. 2018. "Exposure to Nature for Children with Autism Spectrum Disorder: Benefits, Caveats, and Barriers." *Health and Place* 55: 71–79.

Masataka, Nobuo. 2017. "Implications of the Idea of Neurodiversity for Understanding the Origins of Developmental Disorders." *Physics of Life Reviews* 20: 85–108.

Mesibov, Gary B., Victoria Shea, and Eric Schopler. 2004. *The TEACCH Approach to Autism Spectrum Disorders*. New York: Springer.

Wagenfeld, Amy, Marlene Sotelo, and David Kamp. 2019. "Designing an Impactful Sensory Garden for Children and Youth with Autism Spectrum Disorder." *Children, Youth, and Environments* 29(1): 137–152.

Willis, Clarissa. 2006. *Teaching Young Children with Autism Spectrum Disorder*. Lewisville, NC: Gryphon House.

Zachor, Ditza A., et al. 2017. "The Effectiveness of an Outdoor Adventure Programme for Young Children with Autism Spectrum Disorder: A Controlled Study." *Developmental Medicine and Child Neurology* 59(5): 550–556.

CHAPTER 4

Nature as Teacher

I learned from life itself.

— **HELEN KELLER**,
author and disability-rights advocate

The nature-as-teacher concept recognizes the natural environment as a living organism, a place of shared relationships. Nature provides provocations for learning and the materials for generating and investigating ideas. Young children can find unending opportunities for trial-and-error experiments. Nature motivates and inspires; it encourages curiosity and creativity. Nature engages the body, mind, and spirit. It encourages children to test their own instincts and ideas and push beyond their own limits. When educators recognize nature as teacher, they view the natural environment and natural materials as being far more than a setting for activities: nature can play an active role in the learning process.

Nature and children can work together as a child figures out how to accomplish a goal. For example, a child with mobility challenges may want to join other children as they choose a rocky path to get down to a stream. While this child doesn't usually need a mobility device on smooth surfaces, the stamina and balance needed to navigate an uneven terrain may place this child at risk for falling. Before offering to hold the child's hand or suggesting another way down to the creek, you might give the child a chance to do some problem solving. A creative child may find a sturdy stick and use it as a cane for balance. Of course, keep an eye on the child and assist if he asks you to.

In this chapter, we will further explore the concept of nature as teacher with young children with special needs. First, we will look at what nature-based learning is (and is not). Then, we'll discuss why this approach offers so much for children with differing abilities. We'll shine the spotlight on some nature-based programs for children with special needs and illustrate how looking to nature as teacher can promote empathy and caring, as well as more cognitive goals.

Nature-Based Learning

Nature-based learning is an educational approach that recognizes nature as teacher and infuses nature into the educational process. In this approach, children acquire not only knowledge but also skills, values, attitudes, and behaviors. Educators can use nature-based learning in structured group activities, and children can engage in self-determined activities as they act alone or with other children and/or adults.

Nature-based learning is not the same as nature education. *Nature education* means learning about nature and may be an add-on to the curriculum. Nature-based learning may include nature education, but it also goes far beyond that. It involves learning in, for, about, and with nature. A review of the research (Kuo, Barnes, and Jordan, 2019) shows that nature may boost learning through its direct effect on learners, promoting academic learning as well as children's development as persons and as environmental stewards.

Nature supports positive outcomes in eight distinct ways.

- ✿ Restoring attention

- ✿ Reducing stress

- ✿ Improving self-discipline

- ✿ Enhancing motivation, enjoyment, and engagement

- ✿ Increasing levels of physical activity and fitness

- ✿ Helping children feel calmer

- ✿ Fostering cooperative relationships

- ✿ Inviting beneficial forms of play

In their review of the research related to exposure to natural environments and the effects on focused attention, researchers found that exposure to a natural environment improves working memory, attention control, and cognitive flexibility (Stevenson, Schilhab, and Bentsen, 2018).

The restorative power of nature exposure may be especially helpful for children with ADHD who experience greater attention challenges than other children. Research findings show that greater exposure to nature is associated with lower problematic behavior, in particular aggressive behaviors and attention problems, in children with ADHD in both residential and educational settings. Findings relating to educational settings included the idea that spending time outdoors during preschool protects against developing ADHD

~~~~~~

RESEARCH NOTE
GARDEN-BASED LEARNING

Garden-based activities help children learn about science, art and expression, literacy, health and nutrition, the environment, and themselves. One study conducted with teachers at an early childhood education program focused on the effectiveness of garden-based learning for school readiness and for opportunities for autonomy, connectedness, and competence (Murakami, Su-Russell, and Manfra, 2018).

The teachers in this case were working with infants, toddlers, and preschoolers in a learning garden located on the grounds of an early childhood center. In interviews with researchers, they shared their views about the value of and processes for supporting learning among young children in the garden. They identified six school-related readiness areas promoted through garden-based activities:

- Cognition and science
- Physical development
- Social and emotional development
- Understanding of food and nutrition
- Literacy and language skills
- Art and expression

They identified specific garden-related practices, such as participating in garden work, exploring through the senses, and connecting with the community, that they felt supported the children's learning and development. They gave numerous examples of how supporting autonomy, relatedness, and competence can be integrated into garden activities and how garden-based learning can support children's motivation.

In addition to planting and watering, the teachers described other activities such as map making, laying a stepping-stone path, harvesting and eating vegetables, drawing pictures of plants, sharing produce with people in the community, and maintaining a compost pile. Children often chose where, if, and how they wanted to participate. While the educators were actively involved in the activities, they felt it was the children's engagement with the garden itself that promoted autonomy.

in the future (Di Carmine and Berto, 2020; Ulset et al., 2017). For preschoolers experiencing ADHD, play in green settings is associated with less severe attention deficits, and the greener the play area, the stronger the association (Di Carmine and Berto, 2020).

Nature-based learning means more than holding classes outdoors or learning about how to care for the natural environment. In her book *Braiding Sweetgrass: Indigenous Wisdom, Scientific Knowledge, and the Teachings of Plants*, Robin Wall Kimmerer (2013) speaks to the importance of going beyond asking, "What is it?" when learning about nature. She reminds us of the importance of looking to nature for what it can teach us, including learning about the interconnections between humans and the rest of the natural world. Stewardship, or care of the environment, is one aspect of the human-nature connection that is an appropriate area of study for all students. Researchers suggest that a close relationship exists between understanding and caring for one's natural environment and understanding and caring for oneself and others (Schein, 2014). As many children with special needs experience low self-concept, poor social skills, and a learned sense of helplessness, fostering an attitude of stewardship toward the environment may be one way of helping them develop a more positive self-concept, improved relationships with their peers, and a more internal locus of control.

REFLECTIONS: NATURE AS KIN

Nature as teacher is consistent with how young children tend to view and relate to nature. Young children see the environment in relational terms, more as kin than object. It's only as children get older that they begin to view nature as separate from humans.

A kinship way of thinking has implications for educators—especially educators working with young children. A kinship relationship with the natural world isn't defined by knowledge or control. Kinship is fostered when we treat other-than-human living things and their habitats with respect, when we speak of animals and plants as living creatures sharing a common home with all other creatures—both human and nonhuman. Kinship is fostered when we express and encourage taking the perspective of animals, plants, or ecosystems and seeking to understand how they are being affected by circumstances around them.

Nature as kin may have special meaning for children with special needs. The sense of kinship and belonging a child with special needs may feel in and with nature is something he may rarely feel with typically developing peers. Nature invites unscripted interactions. Each child is given the opportunity to play and learn in his own unique way.

Learning with nature includes learning to pull together and for each other. This is how ecosystems work. Learning with nature raises our concerns and interests to a level beyond what is good for the individual self and promotes an understanding of who we are as ecological beings. We are interconnected beings, a part of something much bigger than ourselves.

Kinship with nature is often expressed in warm and caring behaviors. It's not unusual to see such expressions of kinship in young children's spontaneous interactions with elements of nature. Young children want to protect baby trees and may talk to worms in the compost pile. Western pedagogy tends to dismiss such behaviors and focus instead on scientific facts about nature. Learning with nature is based on an appreciation of kinship with nature. Related pedagogy focuses on honoring and deepening the relationship with nature. Kinship with nature is fostered when:

- ✿ children are given unstructured time to be in nature.
- ✿ children are given opportunities to discover similarities between themselves and other living creatures.
- ✿ children spend time caring for other-than-human elements of the natural world.
- ✿ children are given the freedom to explore, to take risks, and to discover that nature is responsive to their presence.
- ✿ children are given the time and space to be in the presence of other living things.
- ✿ children dance with the wind, dig in the dirt, splash in a stream, and taste the sweetness of strawberries fresh off the vine.

Kinship with nature is fostered when children's way of knowing the world is recognized and honored.

Nature-Based Learning and Special Education

Nature-based learning has proven to be effective in promoting the goals of regular education programs. It can also be effective in promoting special-education goals. Nature-based learning lends itself to a variety of direct learning experiences, which are similar to the hands-on direct learning approach that is the foundation of many special-education curricula. Like special education, it emphasizes self-help skills and self-efficacy, individual interests, and skills for fostering quality of life.

Goals and objectives in special education tend to focus on the needs of the whole child rather than exclusively on academic skills. Social, emotional, self-help, and independence goals and objectives are frequently included in a student's IEP, as are goals dealing with the development of appropriate personal and interactional behaviors. Nature-based education takes a similar holistic approach and focuses on the development of the whole child. With nature-based learning, the natural environment provides a setting and materials that are appropriate for all ages, abilities, and areas of learning.

PROGRAM SPOTLIGHT
SEND PROGRAM IN CHINA*

We are a small SEND (Special Educational Needs and Disability) community program serving children ages six to fourteen located in the south of China in Yunnan Province. We are near the famous Mt. Cangshan and Erhai Lake, one of the most beautiful places in the country.

Every week, we spend one and a half days in a natural area to promote children's holistic development. We go hiking, collect trash, explore the forests, and—if it's summer—find a safe stream to wash ourselves and play. Although it's been less than two years since the program was launched, we have already seen huge improvements in the children.

We have one child who showed signs of *mysophobia* (extreme or irrational fear of dirt or contamination) when he entered the program. At home, he was surrounded by six nannies. He became very angry if his clothes got even a tiny bit wet and would ask to be changed immediately. However, he was willing to take off his socks and shoes to go into Erhai Lake. He is delayed in language development and is normally quiet indoors, but the second time we went to the lake, he told us, "I want to play." We were surprised that he used verbal communication. Another day, it started to rain on our way to the mountain, and his shoes and socks were wet. During the two hours it took us to reach the foot of the mountain, he never showed any signs of anger. We assumed nature helped him get over his obsession with being neat and clean.

We've also noticed nature helping other children adapt to different situations and environments. One seven-year-old boy was afraid of insects, especially flying insects such as butterflies and bees. Now, after six months of outdoor exploring, he is much calmer when butterflies come near him.

Another seven-year-old boy with autism was sensitive to sound when he first entered the program. He couldn't stop crying every time we took him to a new place. He kept humming to himself to block out sounds from the environment. After three months of natural play, he's become used to all the different sounds in nature and is able to quietly observe new surroundings. After returning to his home in Shanghai, his mother called to tell us that, for the first time, he seemed comfortable in the urban environment. He likes going outside their apartment and now pays more attention to his surroundings. Before entering our program, he tended to just rush ahead and bump into things with his body. His outdoor explorations taught him to be more cautious, as he had to be careful around sharp stones and spiky plants.

We see examples like these happening every day in our project. We observe children becoming stronger, more adaptive, happy, and willing to immerse themselves in the environment. Nature teaches and challenges the children. They learn to balance their bodies when walking on stones in a stream. Their senses are open and active while engaged with nature. Families report that their children are always excited the day before their scheduled outdoor day and happy afterward. Families also note how the children eat and sleep well after their day outdoors.

*Narrative by Xiuping Yang and Meixi Yan, written by Dr. Huan Chen

Early Childhood Nature-Based Learning

A nature-based approach to education at the early childhood level is not new. Some of the well-known pioneers in the field of early childhood education, including Maria Montessori, Loris Malaguzzi, and Friedrich Froebel, have been strong advocates of nature-based learning.

MARIA MONTESSORI

In the late 1800s, Montessori worked as a physician in a psychiatric clinic in Rome, Italy. She had the opportunity to closely observe children with cognitive challenges. At the time, few if any distinctions were made between cognitive disabilities and insanity. Montessori concluded that educational intervention would be a more effective approach in working with these children than medical treatment would be. She believed that intelligence is not static or fixed but can be influenced by enriching experiences, so she developed an intervention approach that emphasizes sensory activities. This approach proved to be highly effective. Children who were once considered incapable of learning performed successfully on various developmental and academic achievement measures after participating in programs using her approach. While Montessori envisioned child development as a process of natural unfolding, she also believed that environmental influences play a crucial role in how that unfolding occurs.

Montessori recognized nature as a teacher for young children. She believed that nature "offers itself" to the child and that children must have contact with nature (Mooney, 2013).

The Montessori program includes nature engagement as a core element in components of the curriculum: practical life experiences and sensory education. While the practical-life-experiences component includes personal hygiene and self-help skills such as eating and dressing, it also includes motor development, such as walking, climbing, and grasping, as well as responsibility for the natural and built environment, such as caring for plants and animals, raking leaves, and gardening. The sensory-education component focuses on use of the senses and integration of sensory input and is based on the belief that cognitive development is dependent on sensory experiences.

LORIS MALAGUZZI

The Reggio Emilia approach to early childhood education, developed by Loris Malaguzzi, also recognizes the value of nature-based learning for young children. This approach emphasizes the importance of self-expression, cooperation within the community, creativity, and a respect for the natural world (Edwards, Gandini, and Forman, 2011). In her book *Art and Creativity in Reggio Emilia: Exploring the Role and the Potential of Ateliers in Early Childhood Education*, Vea Vecchi (2010) points out that, for children, empathy with surroundings is a kind of natural bridge to a relationship with the environment and is an indispensable basis for relations with others.

Gigi Yu, an assistant professor of art education at the University of New Mexico, and Nora Thompson, a Michigan educator and member of the North American Reggio Emilia Alliance (NAREA), offer the following descriptions of how interaction with nature helps children accept and value differences and care for other beings.

Bird nesting materials

Home for a moth family

> The Reggio Emilia approach promotes an image of all children as being strong, competent, and capable. This is not based on the convocation that all children are the same but rather recognizes and embraces differences as important to the learning context for both the adults and children. In the Reggio Emilia approach, teachers and children welcome, accept, and value differences for the richness they bring to life. There is no "us" or "them," but instead "we," an alliance and concern for one another.
>
> Children often demonstrate this alliance and ability to care for others through their interactions with even the smallest of creatures. We see it occur without suggestion or encouragement. We have witnessed children spontaneously feel inclined to create homes for others, such as leaving nesting materials for birds and imagining a home for a wandering family of moths found on the playground. Children have within them an innate empathy, an understanding of how to relate and take care of others in the world.
>
> Such empathy and understanding were evident in the way children in Nora Thompson's preschool classroom related to a baby chick with facial differences.
>
> Nora's classroom was loaned an incubator with some chicken eggs. When the eggs hatched, the children were filled with joy and wonder and started to notice the subtle differences among the tiny chicks. They noticed that one chick was born with a sideways beak and a missing eye. The children became concerned about whether the chick needed any special care or help due to his

differences. He had some challenges eating at first, so the children moved a small bowl of feed up higher, where the chick did not have to turn his head quite as much to eat. Daily, they talked to him, reassuring him that he could do it. They never made fun of the special chick or treated him like a "less able" chick. Instead, the children cheered him on and celebrated his progress.

The image of children as inclusive and nonjudgmental of creatures within the natural world is one that carries over into how they view and care for each other. The Reggio Emilia approach sees each child as having the right to be accepted for his unique learning style and differences. These differences are not viewed as deficits but as rich learning opportunities for both adults and children in relationship with one another. If we hold an image of a child as capable, full of potential, and possessing a deep interest in caring for others, then we can be confident that, when consulted and listened to, they will teach us about acceptance of differences and empathy.

FRIEDRICH FROEBEL

Froebel, the founder of kindergarten, also played an influential role in helping us understand the benefits of nature for young children. He believed that children's intellectual, moral, and spiritual development were dependent on their relationships with nature. He also believed in children's inherent need to play. Froebel's approach was to engage children in self-directed dialogue with nature, each other, and supportive adult guides. He encouraged children to plant and water seeds, take frequent walks and explore the natural world with their teachers, and explore and experiment with a variety of loose materials. Froebel believed in the concept of nature as teacher. He believed that through nature, children would learn not only about the world around them, but about themselves and their unity with the world as well (Murray, 2018).

In the following vignette, Sandra Duncan, an author and teacher-education consultant, shares some personal experiences and insights about living with a family member with special needs. Some of the lessons she learned may be helpful for teachers working with children with differing abilities.

Susan Virginia Goodwin was an award-winning cherry pie baker, skilled seamstress, church choir member, gardener, and a victim of infantile poliomyelitis—better known as polio. She was also my mom.

Polio is a contagious viral disease that attacks the nervous system and can lead to paralysis and even death. My mom was one of the fortunate people who survived the viral attack but not without suffering multiple physical consequences, including partial paralysis of one arm, spinal-cord weakness, muscle atrophy, and stunted growth of one leg, which caused her to walk with a limp. She was also very small—just a little over four feet tall and weighing ninety pounds.

As a youngster, I remember being ashamed that she was my mom, especially when we were in public. People would point at her, laugh or snicker, and call her names. I especially remember a time someone pointed at her and loudly said, "Hey! Look at that dwarf!" After that, I started walking as far behind her as I could. As often happens when one grows older, I wised up. I would now give anything to be able to take just one walk beside my mom. She died of post-polio syndrome, a well-recognized diagnosis occurring years after polio recovery.

Moms teach us so much about life, and my mom was no exception. She taught me how to cook a pot roast, plant tomato and bean seeds, thread a sewing needle, and balance a checkbook. But perhaps the most important lessons I learned came while fishing with her in a small rowboat on Rice Lake in Wisconsin. These life lessons hold meaning for me as a person and as a teacher.

I learned the importance of being present. When you're in a tiny boat, there's nowhere to hide. I couldn't walk (or sit) behind my mom. As I got older and more mature, I no longer wanted to hide. What mattered was just being with her in the present moment. Today, I realize that being present is also something we need when working with young children, especially children with differing needs and special rights.

I learned the importance of being observant. Because of the paralysis in my mom's arm, she couldn't throw out a fishing line with one of those old-fashioned cane poles. This was no problem for my mom. She just tied a short piece of fishing line to a small tree branch and rigged up a bobber. Then, she would sit completely still and wait for the little water ripples to appear around the sides of the bobber. Moments later, she would be pulling up a fish. Today, I realize that being observant is exactly what we need to do as educators of young children. We need to be as mindful and respectful of what's below the surface—emotions, feelings— as we are about what we can see—behaviors and actions. This is especially important for children with disabilities.

A third lesson I learned relates to what we celebrate. On days when we caught only very small fish, my mom celebrated the biggest fish we caught. I believe the same should be true when working with children with differing abilities. There may be times when we fail to catch the "big one," but there is always something we can celebrate.

Nature-Based Learning Today

Nature-based learning is receiving increased attention at all levels of education, especially at the early childhood level. Before 2000, I found it difficult to find more than ten nature-based preschools in the United States. By 2017, there were approximately two hundred seventy-five such programs. Just three years later, the number of such preschools in the United States was estimated to be close to six hundred programs (Natural Start Alliance, 2020).

Related research has also increased dramatically. A recent search of the Children & Nature Network (C&NN) Research Library found fifty-seven studies tagged as "nature kindergarten/preschool/ forest school." Fifty-two of the studies were published between 2016 and 2019. Because the research library is relatively new—it was launched in 2015—it's difficult to know how much research looked at nature-based preschools before that time. However, a search of the academic literature for related articles published from 2012 through 2015 identified only twenty studies; a search covering the four years prior to that (2008–2011) identified just four.

Research conducted around the world provides a strong evidence-based rationale for nature-based learning at the early childhood level. This research can be accessed through the C&NN Research Library (https://research.childrenandnature.org/research-library/) and the research hub of the North American Association of Environmental Education (NAAEE) https://naaee.org/eepro/research/library). Both short- and long-term nature-based programs have proven effective in promoting child development and learning (Dankiw et al., 2020; Kuo, Barnes, and Jordan, 2019). They've also proven effective in supporting children's biophilia or affinity for nature (Barrable and Booth, 2020; Lithoxoidou et al., 2017).

But do nature-based preschools prepare children for kindergarten? A recent study addressed this question (Cordiano et al., 2019). The researchers compared assessment results of two groups of students with similar backgrounds attending the same school. One group participated in a traditional, high-quality prekindergarten program; the other group participated in a new, nature-based prekindergarten program. Children in the nature-based program spent 90 percent of their school day, five days per week, outdoors on the school's campus. Children in the traditional program spent one morning per week and one immersion week in the spring in the outdoor environment; this group stayed indoors the rest of the time. Teachers for both classes used the same curriculum. Results showed that children in both types of preschool programs achieved expected developmental gains in their early academic skills and their social-emotional functioning over the year prior to kindergarten. These results indicate that nature-based preschools can be just as effective in promoting academic and social-emotional goals as programs delivered in a more traditional environment.

Early childhood nature-based learning takes a variety of forms—from forest schools, where children spend the entire school day in the same outdoor environment, to mobile preschools, where children ride a bus to different natural areas on a daily basis. There are, of course, many other variations at the early childhood level, including family nature clubs and occasional visits to nature centers.

In addition to the rapid growth in nature-based preschools, another indication of growing interest in nature-based learning is the development of teacher-preparation programs combining nature and early learning. Currently, only a handful of such programs exist, but a number of colleges and universities are in the process of developing undergraduate and graduate courses of study preparing professionals to work in a variety of nature-based preschool settings (based on the author's personal communication with Yash Bhagwanji, Florida Atlantic University; David Sobel, Antioch New England University; and Patty Born Selly, Hamline University).

Some institutions of higher education and professional organizations are also offering in-service courses on nature-based learning at the early childhood level. While the preservice and in-service offerings can differ in focus and intensity, almost all are based on the idea that the benefits of nature-based learning apply to young children, their families, society, and the environment.

The benefits children gain from outdoor explorations and play can vary considerably. One benefit relates to how other people view children with special needs. The following section illustrates not only how the behaviors of some children improve once they get outdoors but also how their functioning in an outdoor environment allows others to note their capabilities versus disabilities.

The Child Outdoors

Families and teachers sometimes note how children with challenging behaviors tend to be different when playing outdoors. Indoors, a child may be reckless with materials, uncooperative, and aggressive with others. Outdoors, the same child may be protective of worms and a willing participant in building a fort or designing a raft for crossing a stream. Children labeled as "under-achieving" in the classroom can be leaders and risk-takers in the outdoors.

Teachers from eight schools in the United Kingdom worked with researchers Trisha Maynard, Jane Waters, and Jennifer Clement (2013) over a one-year period. They looked at the effects of the outdoor environment on forty-eight children who were identified as "underachieving" socially, emotionally, or academically in the normal classroom environment. The children with social difficulties generally found it hard to relate to peers in the classroom. The children with emotional difficulties tended to be shy or withdrawn; and the children with academic difficulties generally performed poorly in literacy or numeracy.

All the teachers were trained to use child-initiated learning in their school's outdoor environment. Outdoor activities included free play with natural resources, such as leaves, sticks, sand, and water; vegetable gardening; problem-solving activities, such as building an enclosure for ducks; and structured investigations of natural elements and phenomena, such as snails, air and wind, and flight.

Observations indicated that the natural outdoor spaces where child-led activities took place fostered child-initiated learning and diminished teachers' perceptions of children as underachieving. The children appeared to come into their own and were able to see themselves as strong and competent rather than as underachieving students. Case studies produced by the teachers indicated that at least 50 percent of the children they had identified as underachieving made important gains in self-control, concentration, social interaction, perseverance, conflict management, and self-confidence.

As these findings indicate, perceived underachievement diminished or disappeared. In some cases, this effect might be explained by the fact that, in the outdoor environment, some behaviors, such as boisterous behavior, or characteristics are not seen as problematic as they would be indoors. The behaviors may not have changed, but the context in which they occurred led to different interpretations of the behaviors by the teachers. Some teachers were able to see underachievement as a product of the learning environment or context, and they viewed behaviors and performance more than the characteristics and capability of the individual child. They recognized the effects of outdoor environments and child-led learning on positive changes in behavior and performance, such as increased concentration on task, increased engagement and enjoyment, a willingness to help others and share ideas, fewer squabbles, and more attentive listening.

According to the teachers, children with special needs seemed to have more of an equal footing with other children when they were outdoors. They were given more opportunities to show and share their expertise with other children.

The discussion in this chapter recognized nature as teacher in the lives of young children with varying abilities. This idea is consistent with what early childhood educators have long understood—that the environment is an important contributor to young children's development and learning. The next chapter, which highlights nature as healer, presents information and personal stories about children (and teachers) experiencing nature as a source of solace, inspiration, and joy.

REFERENCES

Barrable, Alexia, and David Booth. 2020. "Increasing Nature Connection in Children: A Mini Review of Interventions." *Frontiers in Psychology.* https://doi.org/10.3389/fpsyg.2020.00492

Cordiano, Tori S., et al. 2019. "Nature-Based Education and Kindergarten Readiness: Nature-Based and Traditional Preschoolers Are Equally Prepared for Kindergarten." *International Journal of Early Childhood Environmental Education* 6(3): 18–36.

Dankiw, Kylie A., et al. 2020. "The Impacts of Unstructured Nature Play on Health in Early Childhood Development: A Systematic Review." *PLoS ONE* 15(2). https://doi.org/10.1371/journal.pone.0229006

Di Carmine, Francesca, and Rita Berto. 2020. "Contact with Nature Can Help ADHD Children to Cope with Their Symptoms: The State of the Evidence and Future Directions for Research." *Visions for Sustainability.* doi: https://doi.org/10.13135/2384-8677/4883

Edwards, Carolyn, Lella Gandini, and George Forman. 2011. *The Hundred Languages of Children: The Reggio Emilia Experience in Transformation.* 3rd edition. Westport, CT: Praeger.

Kimmerer, Robin Wall. 2013. *Braiding Sweetgrass: Indigenous Wisdom, Scientific Knowledge, and the Teachings of Plants.* Minneapolis, MN: Milkweed Editions.

Kuo, Ming, Michael Barnes, and Catherine Jordan. 2019. "Do Experiences with Nature Promote Learning? Converging Evidence of a Cause-and-Effect Relationship." *Frontiers in Psychology* 10: 305. doi:10.3389/fpsyg.2019.00305

Lithoxoidou, Loukia S., Alexandros D. Georgopoulos, Anastasia Th. Dimitriou, Sofia Ch. Xenitidou. 2017. "'Trees Have a Soul Too!' Developing Empathy and Environmental Values in Early Childhood." *The International Journal of Early Childhood Environmental Education* 5(1): 68–88.

Maynard, Trisha, Jane Waters, and Jennifer Clement. 2013. "Child-Initiated Learning, the Outdoor Environment, and the Underachieving Child." *Early Years* 33(3): 212–225.

Mooney, Carol Gerhart. 2013. *Theories of Childhood: An Introduction to Dewey, Montessori, Erikson, Piaget, and Vygotsky*. St. Paul, MN: Redleaf.

Murakami, Christopher D., Chang Su-Russell, and Louis Manfra. 2018. "Analyzing Teacher Narratives in Early Childhood Garden-Based Education." *Journal of Environmental Education* 49(1): 18–29.

Murray, Jane. 2018. "Value/s in Early Childhood Education." *International Journal of Early Years Education* 26(3): 215–219.

Natural Start Alliance. 2020. Natural Start Alliance Map. Natural Start Alliance. https://naturalstart.org/map?field_organization_type_value=A+licensed+preschool+or+childcare+facility

Schein, Deborah. 2014. "Nature's Role in Children's Spiritual Development." *Children, Youth and Environments* 24(2): 78–101.

Stevenson, Matt, Theresa Schilhab, and Peter Bentsen. 2018. "Attention Restoration Theory II: A Systematic Review to Clarify Attention Processes Affected by Exposure to Natural Environments." *Journal of Toxicology and Environmental Health, Part B*. 21(4): 227–268.

Ulset, Vidar, et al. 2017. "Time Spent Outdoors During Preschool: Links with Children's Cognitive and Behavioral Development." *Journal of Environmental Psychology* 52: 69–80.

Vecchi, Vea. 2010. *Art and Creativity in Reggio Emilia: Exploring the Role and the Potential of Ateliers in Early Childhood Education*. New York: Routledge.

CHAPTER 5

Nature as Healer

"

There is something infinitely healing
in the repeated refrains of nature.

— **RACHEL CARSON,**
marine biologist, author, and conservationist

Helen Keller, blind and deaf due to a childhood illness, speaks in her writings of "ecstatic mornings" wandering in the fields with her teacher. She, of course, is unable to see with her eyes and hear with her ears, yet Keller experiences the beauty of wildflowers and senses the sounds of the earth. These experiences, which she writes about in *The World I Live In and Optimism* (1903/1908), bring her great joy. Keller's descriptions of what nature-related experiences meant to her are similar to what Rachel Carson writes in *The Sense of Wonder* (1956): "Those who contemplate the beauty of the earth find reserves of strength that will endure as long as life lasts."

The Healing Balm of Nature

Helen Keller and Rachel Carson describe what many of us experience as the healing balm of nature. Humans often turn to nature for rejuvenation, as we find that nature has a way of calming our troubled spirits. We may go for a hike, go camping over a long weekend, or spend several hours in our garden. Some people turn to a practice that the Japanese call *shinrin-yoku* or "forest bathing," which involves walking in the woods. It is based on the idea of "taking in the forest atmosphere." Researchers, health-care professionals, and even some governments now recognize the healing potential of *shinrin-yoku*. While this practice is associated with physical health benefits, including improved immune-system functioning and reduced blood pressure, the mental-health benefits may be felt immediately (Tsunetsugu, Park, and Miyazaki, 2010; Hansen, Jones, and Tocchini, 2017). Physically taking in the forest atmosphere relates to the way trees and other plants emit certain organic compounds (phytoncides) that we inhale. These compounds increase our immune-system functioning. The mental health benefits relate more to uplifted spirits—we feel more relaxed and less stressed when we walk through a forest. But Helen Keller and Rachel Carson seem to be referring to something else—to some enduring benefits that enrich our lives over time and are carried in our memories and our spirits. As we take in the forest atmosphere, we do more than ingest organic compounds. We take in sensory impressions as well, such as the sound of water running over pebbles or the feel of soft blossoms against our cheek. Taking in sensory impressions is a function of our minds and hearts, not just our bodies.

Time in nature with children, perhaps especially children with special needs, is full of engagement and golden opportunities to pause in wonder and stand in awe. Teachers who work in outdoor nature classrooms report that the children tend to be more engaged with materials and other people outside than they are in indoors (Dennis, Kiewra, and Wells, 2019). In the following, researcher and assistant professor Christine Kiewra reflects on her experiences of children's awe and wonder in nature.

> When I was a preschool teacher, Brandon, a four-year-old with autism, taught me firsthand about awe and wonder in nature. I noticed that, indoors, Brandon often ensured furniture (usually a table or shelf) was between him and his classmates, making both conversation and eye contact rare. Brandon appeared trapped, uneasy, and detached.

In contrast, outdoor time for Brandon consistently began with a solo walk along the path through the garden and a pause to pet his favorite plant, a lamb's ear (*Stachys byzantina*). Frequently after his stroll, Brandon settled in to closely observe an insect, dig a hole in the soil, or roll heavy logs into place to build a fort. Often other children and I investigated alongside Brandon. We were drawn together through the discoveries of unearthed worms from deep below the surface, fascinating insect trails on decaying logs, and the birds Brandon was able to spot soaring high above long before we ever could. I came to understand that Brandon, and many other children, benefitted from time to wander and the freedom to choose. I was often in awe of the discoveries Brandon uncovered. Free to engage with materials and people on his own terms, Brandon revealed his gifts, not just his challenges, to all of us.

As I became involved with Dimensions Foundation natural outdoor classroom research, my colleagues and I continued to learn from observing children outdoors. In our paper "Playing with Nature: Supporting Preschoolers' Creativity in Natural Outdoor Classrooms" (Kiewra and Veselack, 2016), we note children's capacity for deep focus and sustained attention when their play is meaningful to them and they have time to formulate, process, engage, evaluate, trouble-shoot, construct, rethink, rework, and discover. We stated, "This is where the true learning takes place, when the child's brain is engaged and working hard." We also note the importance of giving children lots of uninterrupted time: "Large blocks of time allow children to go deeper in their exploratory processes resulting in creative problem-solving and original ideas, freeing the mind of the young child to ponder and dream, to think over a problem critically and try a variety of solutions. . . ." These activities help a child learn and grow the capacity for flexible and divergent thinking.

In my role as a teacher educator, I more fully recognize the benefits of time in nature not solely for children but for teachers as well. As my college students learn to closely observe and join in play with children outdoors, they recognize the power of nature. They learn to appreciate that spending time in natural outdoor classrooms can enhance their receptiveness to children's ideas and, in turn, their effectiveness as teachers.

A survey of educators with natural outdoor classrooms showed that time in natural spaces left teachers "always" or "most of the time" feeling refreshed and patient and, therefore, more likely to respond sensitively to children and ready to give them the individual attention they need (Dennis, Kiewra, and Wells, 2019). I often share the sentiment from Dr. Ruth Wilson's book *Learning Is in Bloom: Cultivating Outdoor Explorations* that teachers do not need to choose between education and enchantment—we can have both. Nature affords children and teachers opportunities to experience awe and wonder when we embrace learning together.

One of the secret ingredients in outdoor learning may be how nature supports feelings of calm and tranquility. Reduction in stress levels in children and teachers supports our ability to be truly present in the moment with each other. When adults and children are in step, positive interactions lead to bonds of trust that support learning. Joining in the "flow" with preschoolers empowers children to make decisions about their own learning and emboldens teachers to trust children's choices. These joyful moments can enable all of us, no matter our age or abilities, to come to a deeper sense of our unique selves, the gifts we have to share, and our place in the universe. Isn't that what education is all about?

"Being" in nature enriches children's life in the moment and has "the capacity to motivate children to continue to seek out nature as they grow" (Beery, Chawla, and Levin, 2020). The healing balm of nature is something children can experience in the present, but it is also something children can carry with them over time. This aspect of the experience contributes to their "becoming." "Becoming" in nature helps children learn adult roles in caring for the natural environment. The "becoming" aspect of children's engagement can also relate to a child's holistic development. Both the "being" and "becoming" aspects may be especially beneficial for children with special needs because these children tend to experience greater physical, social, and/or emotional challenges in developing life skills and achieving academic success than their typically developing peers. Dealing with these challenges can be physically and emotionally exhausting, so children with special needs may have a greater need for rest and relaxation than other children.

Crista, a literacy coach and licensed special educator, describes how nature has become a healing balm for her son, Nate:

Engaging in the outside natural world seems to calm and quiet my son's mind. But it wasn't always like this. In addition to Down syndrome, Nate has developmental and health issues that affect how he navigates his days. Now twelve, Nate didn't walk until he was four years old. Once he started walking, he still avoided uneven ground, expressing worry that he could fall. He was also a child with so many sensory sensitivities that the things many people love—such as grass and sand—were things that felt untouchable to him.

I recall summer trips to the ocean where I watched children all around us running back and forth to the water with their buckets as they excitedly built sand creations. In contrast, Nate would pull his legs up completely perpendicular to the sand to avoid feeling those coarse, hot grains touching his body. I would slowly pour sand over his feet and carry him to the water to gently dip his toes into an incoming wave of ocean water to give him these experiences in ways he could tolerate.

Recently, I observed Nate watching his neighborhood friend make mud pies. Across the fence, she was in her yard explaining to him how to use water to make the mud just the right consistency. I brought Nate a pan, a bucket of dirt, and a jar of water. Nate watched his friend carefully as she modeled and taught him this new way to engage in the outside world. Soon they were collecting daffodils to garnish their creations. While engaging in nature may be intuitive for some, it was something Nate needed to be taught, and I realized that the best teacher for this would be a friend.

After surgery to correct a serious hip issue, Nate is now able to walk independently. In the midst of the COVID-19 pandemic, our family started taking walks every day. This daily afternoon ritual helped us stay grounded during this challenging time. Nate even started walking to a "sit spot" by himself in the woods on our property. At times, my husband,

Eric, and I have allowed Nate to go into the woods on his own for up to 15 or 20 minutes. Although Nate has started to venture farther, he is always safe and often with his dog, Josie.

One day, after Nate had been gone longer than usual, we went to look for him at his sit spot. He wasn't there. Sheer panic flooded us, and we started calling frantically for him. Following our usual path, we found Nate proudly returning to the house. In that split second, we had to choose how to respond. The look on Nate's face communicated that he was proud that he did this walk in nature all by himself. We realized that his comfort and confidence in nature had given him a gift— the opportunity to experience his world with independence.

RESEARCH NOTE
NATURE AS REFUGE

A recent study investigated how young children attending an early child-care program experience relaxation (Cooke et al., 2020). Forty-six children ages three to five years from six child-care programs in Brisbane, Australia, participated in group interviews. They were asked to tell or show what it means to relax and what they do to relax. Many children described relaxation as being sensory rich and included feelings of being cozy and comfy. They identified place and play as important factors in their experience of relaxation. Their most common places for experiencing relaxation were in nature and at home. Some children found playing quietly alone to be relaxing; others described playing with friends as relaxing.

In describing nature as a place for relaxation, children made numerous references to watching, touching, and feeling nature. They talked about how looking at trees and lying in soft grass made them feel happy and relaxed. These findings are consistent with other research, in which children indicated that they looked to nature as a refuge in dealing with pressures in their lives. Observing beauty in nature, listening to birds, and feeling the wind are examples of stress-reducing experiences for young children. Such experiences are sometimes referred to as being restorative. *Restoration,* in this context, refers to the renewal of adaptive resources, such as the ability to inhibit impulses and regain a positive mood, that have become depleted in meeting the demands and stressors of everyday life.

For children to enjoy the healing balm of nature, they need access to natural places. Limited opportunities to "be" and "become" in nature (Beery, Chawla, and Levin, 2020) can have negative lasting effects. As discussed in chapter 2, children with special needs tend to have fewer experiences in nature than their typically developing peers and are missing many of the health-related benefits of engagement with nature.

Environmental psychologist Louise Chawla has studied the types of places and experiences that stay in our memories and influence who we become as adults. Her work highlights the importance of childhood experiences in nature-rich environments. She describes such experiences as giving children "ecstatic memories," which can sustain and delight them over time (Chawla, 1990). According to Chawla, "We do not need to consciously preserve these memories; we know that we can never lose them. They are like radioactive jewels buried within us, emitting energy across the years of our lives." Chawla's findings are consistent with the insights offered by Helen Keller and Rachel Carson. Nature-related experiences during childhood and ways in which these experiences foster connectedness to nature can enrich a child's life in both the present and the future. Some of the research on the mental health benefits of nature exposure during childhood suggests that such exposure can even make children less likely to experience mental health problems during adulthood (Engemann et al., 2019).

Allyson, Leela's mother, has seen firsthand how nature-related experiences in her daughter's early childhood years have fostered Leela's connectedness to nature and have had a healing effect.

Leela was born with Down syndrome and, from birth, had some hearing and vision challenges. She had open-heart surgery when she was two months old to patch congenital defects. She has chronic kidney disease, hypothyroidism, and partial agenesis (failure of all or a part of an organ to form or develop) of the corpus callosum, which connects the two hemispheres of the brain. Leela is now five years old and doing well as a kindergartener at the New Mexico School for the Deaf (NMSD).

A unique aspect of the NMSD program is a Forest Day Learning (FDL) experience. Leela has been a part of this program since she was three years old. Allyson has seen ways in which the nature-rich experiences have been good for Leela—nature is a teacher, therapist, and source of joy for her.

While time in nature has helped Leela learn about her physical self, it has also helped her learn about her spirit, her soul. Allyson notices how Leela readily taps into the changes of the seasons and the movements of the wind. "Nature, for Leela," she says, "is a living organism, a place of shared relationship." Allyson describes Leela's experience as "being with nature versus doing something in or to nature . . . Leela seems to have a sense of belonging in nature. It has a calming effect on her." Allyson describes how the sensory elements of nature can, at times, allow for a sensory reset. "Tantrums end when we take Leela outside. It's a healing-in-the-moment experience." According to Allyson, Leela's experiences with nature have elevated her sense of self, allowing her to see herself as a part of something larger. She gives the example of how Leela moved from touching and observing ants and other living creatures to developing a respectful curiosity for the world of nature.

Protecting Leela's health has always been a primary consideration in any activities outside the house—school, play dates, outings, and so on. Balancing the ever-present health concerns with the need for socializing and play has always been a challenge. This becomes especially difficult in winter, when Leela faces intense and life-threatening battles with viruses and flu. Her parents recognize the value of exploring outside in a natural environment where transmission is far less risky. Outdoors, Leela can play like all the other kids and experience the many benefits nature has to offer.

Allyson describes how the therapeutic benefits of nature extend to their entire family. As Leela develops confidence and a greater sense of independence, the family enjoys more time together outdoors. "We experience shared joy and a shared communion with nature. This is something we all need."

Stress Reduction Theory

Some of the mental-health benefits associated with nature engagement relate to the experience of being away from the stressors of daily life, an idea expressed in the generally accepted stress reduction theory (SRT), which is supported by an impressive body of research. SRT is based on the idea that viewing vegetation and other natural-appearing environmental features can evoke positive emotions that block negative thoughts and emotions. There are some indications that reducing stress in the moment may also serve as a buffer against the development of mental illness in the future (Bratman et al., 2015).

More and more hospitals and health-care facilities across the country are tapping into the benefits of nature. While "healing gardens" may come to mind as a nature-focused component of some hospitals, other ways of incorporating nature as an aid for healing include natural lighting, nature-related art, and the presence of plants and animals. These nature-focused elements may be found more often in pediatric healthcare facilities than in other hospital settings.

Health-care professionals understand that healing spaces for children are more than a place where children receive medical treatments. Children need emotional nurturing for healing. Connection to nature can promote the healing process by serving as a buffer between life stressors and psychological distress. Related research indicates that direct or even indirect access to nature can reduce pain and stress and may even give patients an increased sense of control in health-care environments (Gaminiesfahani, Lozanovska, and Tucker, 2020). Indirect access includes viewing natural elements, such as trees, flowers, fountains, and bird feeders, through a window, having plants in the room, and seeing images of nature. Direct access to nature includes interaction with animals and playing with natural materials, such as shells, stones, and pine cones.

RESEARCH NOTE
DISH GARDENS FOR HEALING

"Healing gardens" are typically found outside health-care facilities. Some patients, however, may not be able to access such gardens. One alternative is to use dish gardens in hospital rooms. A dish garden is an indoor miniature garden that includes vegetation, rocks, water features, and mulches.

Yar and Kazemi (2020) investigated the role of dish gardens on the physical and neuropsychological improvement of hospitalized children. In a hospital in Iran, fifty-four children ages six to fifteen were randomly assigned to a hospital room with a dish garden or a hospital room without a dish garden.

Before exposure to the dish gardens, the physical and neuropsychological indices of the two groups of children were not significantly different. The children who were assigned to a room with a dish garden, however, later had significantly lower blood pressure and respiration rates than children without a dish garden. Children with a dish garden in their room also experienced less fear, anxiety, and depression and more happiness and relaxation than the children without a dish garden.

Nature-Nurture Programs

Different agencies around the world are developing programs based on the idea that nature can be effective in promoting the holistic development of children, including children with special needs. The "Encounter in Nature" program in Israel is one example. "Encounter in Nature" is a nature therapy program for primary-age children with learning difficulties and/or special needs. In this program, a therapist and a teacher conduct sessions in natural spaces, such as small groves, parks, or gardens, within or near school grounds for two hours a week throughout the school year. The therapeutic educational program focuses on empowering the students, not on "fixing" them but helping them become all that they can become. Activities include storytelling, outdoor challenges, adventure games, art activities, and nature-conservation projects.

Since the founding of the program in 2002, hundreds of schoolchildren from the entire special-needs spectrum (developmental delays, autism, learning difficulties, ADHD, ADD, severe behavioral and emotional disorders) have participated. The program has been shown to help the children develop self-esteem and self-confidence (Berger, 2020).

The Nature Nurture program in Scotland is another example of a nature-based therapeutic program for children experiencing stress and trauma. The primary aim of Nature Nurture is to help young children from challenging home environments develop resilience. Through nature, nurture, and free play—the three main components of the program—children are helped to develop the skills needed to maintain appropriate functioning despite significant emotional adversity.

A related study (McArdle, Harrison, and Harrison, 2013) focused on children ages four and five who participated in the Nature Nurture program one afternoon per week over a period of ten weeks. Program activities included walks in the woods, collecting "treasures" in nature, and playing at different stations set up in the woods. These stations encouraged physical activity, exploration, and creating crafts. Assessments conducted with the children over the ten-week period showed progress in several areas of development including emotional stability, dealing with stress, self-control, and thoughtfulness. The behavior of some of the children would have made it difficult for them to participate in a regular classroom setting. The woods provided a safe environment in which learning linked to resilience could occur. The balance between structure and freedom provided by the program seemed just right for promoting children's confidence, problem-solving skills, and willingness to take small risks. Something about the permanence and predictability of the natural environment seemed to have a calming and comforting effect on the children. Researchers McArdle, Harrison, and Harrison concluded that the nurturing and positive approach contributed to the development of the following resilient personality factors:

- Increased confidence in the face of new challenges
- Self-control
- Empathy
- Motivation
- Focus
- Perseverance

The researchers noted that the natural setting provided children with new challenges and the opportunity to take safe risks and also contributed to increased calm and relaxation.

Nature-Based Therapy

The term *therapy* is often used in reference to treatments or interventions intended to treat or heal an injury or illness, but therapy can also be used in reference to prevention. We may get a flu vaccine, for example, to prevent getting the flu. One of the clear messages we get from reading Richard Louv's book *Last Child in the Woods* is that increasing children's engagement with nature may prevent them from experiencing what Louv calls "nature-deficit disorder." Louv provides multiple examples of how engaging children with nature can prevent or reduce symptoms associated with nature-deficit disorder, including diminished uses of the senses and attention difficulties.

Other experts offer similar messages. Clemens Arvay, in *The Healing Code of Nature,* for example, calls attention to the many physical and mental therapeutic effects of nature on humans. He describes how many natural elements, such as trees, bodies of water, birds and birdsong, and berry bushes, provide stimuli for our overall health and for activating our biophilic forces.

Nature for healing isn't exactly a new concept. An article published in *The American Journal of Public Health* (Crnic and Kondo, 2019) describes how prescriptions for the therapeutic use of nature were popular in some US cities in the late nineteenth and early twentieth centuries. These programs typically served children with health concerns such as being underweight and conditions such as polio and tuberculosis. The objectives of these programs varied widely from providing a safe place for children to play to treating seriously ill infants and children. The programs were based on the idea that time outdoors was beneficial to children's health and well-being. Despite their popularity, these and other nature-based therapeutic programs gradually faded from medical practice during the 20th century and were replaced with more clinical practices.

Recently, there's been a re-emergence of pediatric nature-based programs, with physicians and other health-care professionals showing more interest in programs providing urban children with increased access to nature. These programs—referred to as "nature prescription" or "park prescription" programs—focus on concerns related to ailments associated with a more sedentary and indoor lifestyle, such as overweight and obesity, ADHD, anxiety, and depression.

Nature-based therapy is sometimes referred to as *ecotherapy*. First used by Howard Clinebell in his book *Ecotherapy: Healing Ourselves, Healing the Earth*, ecotherapy is a form of "ecological spirituality," suggesting that a holistic relationship with nature encompasses both nature's ability to nurture us and our ability to reciprocate. Both sides of this equation are known to offer healing.

Nature-based therapy applies ecopsychology to emotional healing. Professionals adopting this form of therapy are sometimes referred to as *ecotherapists* and intentionally use the benefits of the natural world to promote healing and growth. With nature-based therapy, nature is much more than a setting for the therapy; it is a catalyst for the therapeutic process that takes place in the interaction between the individual and the natural environment. Nature as healer—like nature as teacher—recognizes the natural environment as a place of shared relationships. Nature can help a child feel welcomed, competent, courageous, calm, and happy.

John La Puma, a board-certified internist, is a strong advocate of nature therapy. La Puma (2019) describes nature therapy as the prescriptive, evidence-based use of natural settings and nature-based interventions for the purpose of preventing certain clinical conditions and promoting well-being. Nature therapy can take many different forms, including animal-assisted therapy (see chapter 9), care farms, forest bathing, and horticultural therapy (see chapter 10).

The importance of making ecotherapy interventions available for children is highlighted by the fact that as many as 50 percent of lifetime cases of mental illness begin by age fourteen (Roberts, Hinds, and Camic, 2019). The rate of mental-health problems in people with autism and some other forms of disability is greater than that of the general population. Some of the likely reasons for this disparity include a higher incidence of negative life events, fewer coping skills, and the effects of other people's attitudes. These factors place people with special needs at risk for increased anxiety, depression, and psychological distress (Mesibov, Shea, and Schopler, 2004).

We can broadly categorize nature-based interventions for improvements in health and well-being into those that change the environment and those that change behavior. Changing the environment incorporates such initiatives as providing gardens in hospitals and parks in cities, as well as adding nature-related items to indoor settings, such as images of nature (photos, videos, paintings, and so on) or real natural elements (indoor green plants, flowers, and wooden materials).

Interventions designed to change behavior include such nature-related programs as park prescriptions and wilderness therapy. These interventions are designed for people of all ages— preschool through elderly adults—and focus on a broad range of physical, mental, emotional, and social health-related outcomes.

CHILD-CENTERED NATURE-BASED THERAPY

The natural physical space and materials play important roles in child-centered nature-based therapy. The child needs to feel safe in the outdoor setting and have the opportunity to interact freely with nature. Vegetation in the natural space adds interest and promotes exploration. Many children will use plant parts and other natural materials for pretend play. As the child explores and plays, the therapist may look for demonstrations of nurturance, such as watering plants, and a willingness to try new things, such as digging holes in the dirt or climbing a tree. The therapist may also look for ways that a child responds to limits set by the therapist. For example, a therapist may be okay with a child using a stick for drumming but not okay with throwing the stick high into the air.

Some children respond to nature-based therapy by becoming more aware of happenings in the natural environment. They may, for example, notice the sun shining on the trunk of a tree, birds singing nearby, and leaves moving in the breeze. Noticing and connecting with the natural environment can be soothing for the child. This, in turn, can help the child become more cooperative and communicative during the therapy session and may carry over into other settings and situations. In addition to decreased symptoms of ADHD, other positive results include higher self-esteem, greater empathy, and feelings of empowerment.

Certain situations, such as inclement weather, the need for privacy, allergies, and the lack of nearby nature, sometimes serve as barriers to the outdoor option, so nature-based therapy can also occur indoors. A recent study conducted by Jacqueline Swank and colleagues (2020) asked professionals about their counseling practices and found that 69 percent use natural elements within their indoor counseling space. The clinicians used elements such as natural sounds; guided imagery involving nature; and technologically simulated, delivered, or enhanced nature. According to the clinicians, positive results for their clients included greater focus, new insights, and feeling more creative and relaxed.

Integrated Therapies

At times, nature-based therapy is integrated with other forms of therapy, such as art therapy, music therapy, and drama therapy.

THE EFFECTS OF NATURE ON YOUNG CHILDREN

Research shows the positive effects access to green space can have on the mental well-being of children. In her review of the research, Rachel McCormick (2017) concluded that the evidence demonstrating the mental-health benefits of nature for children can guide policy and urban planning. The evidence also showed that nursing interventions and initiatives that promote outdoor play, educate patients and families, advocate for recess and green environments at school, and encourage healing gardens in hospital settings can enhance children's health, especially for children with ADHD and other behavioral concerns.

In her book *Balanced and Barefoot*, Angela Hanscom notes that as children play outdoors they build confidence and learn to be adaptable. Nature is therapeutic, she says, in the multiple ways in which it stimulates the senses and sets children up for healthy sensory integration.

Researchers from the University of Florida (Swank et al., 2015) examined the effect of a child-centered nature-based therapy approach with early elementary school children who exhibited behavioral problems. Counselors trained in nature-based therapy worked with each child twice a week in an outdoor natural environment. Results showed a decrease in behavior problems and an increase in on-task behaviors for participants with and without ADHD, even after the seven-week program ended.

ART THERAPY

Making a large-group collage using natural materials is one way to integrate art therapy with nature-based therapy. For a large-group collage, each child can contribute something that she or he discovered in the natural environment, such as a stone, leaf, or seed pod, and place it on a large piece of cardboard or in a designated area in the sand, grass, dirt, or forest floor.

A related activity involves the creation of nicho boxes, which are art boxes inspired by wall niches common to Southwestern architecture, termed *nichos*. Each nicho contains small objects that reflect a person's identity, culture, or interests. Children can create nicho boxes to express their relationship to a place or to show what is important to them in the natural environment. They can paint or cover their box with paper and then arrange natural objects, little figurines of people or animals, photographs, or pictures cut from magazines—anything that the children find meaningful to express themselves and their relationship to the environment—in the box with glue or a glue gun (with adult help).

MUSIC THERAPY

Because nature sounds—bird song, moving water, and wind through various plants, for example—are generally pleasing to people, it's not surprising to find nature sounds integrated into settings where music therapy is used. Nature sounds tend to have a calming effect on people. While research done from the music-therapy perspective is scarce, virtually all existing literature on the use of nature sounds to reduce anxiety and induce relaxed states indicates that nature sounds are uniquely effective in accomplishing these goals. Whether applied before, during, or after a stressful event, natural sounds can have a noticeable effect on reducing anxiety and promoting a relaxed state (Largo-Wight, O'Hara, and Chen, 2016).

Nature therapy and music can also be integrated by offering music classes, lessons, or performances outdoors in a natural environment, as is done in the therapeutic garden at the Els Center of Excellence in Jupiter, Florida. (See the Program Spotlight on page 46.) Another way to integrate nature therapy and music is to add musical instruments and/or wind chimes to a natural play space where adults can conduct therapy sessions. Teachers can make or purchase xylophones and drums designed for outdoor weather; encouraging children to make their own musical instruments from natural materials is also a good idea. For example, a child using a stick to strike the trunks of trees discovered that every tree has a different sound.

Many people, including children, find that attending to the music of nature can be therapeutic. Gentle sounds made by birds, water, rain, and wind can be soothing and calming.

DRAMA THERAPY

Ronen Berger, coauthor of *The Healing Forest in Post-Crisis Work with Children* (2013), has used integrated nature therapy with different school groups and children of different ages—often with children who have experienced trauma.

One form of nature therapy discussed by Berger (2020) uses nature as the stage for dramatic-creative activity. Another form takes drama therapy or other arts-related therapies outside into nature. As Berger explains, nature therapy can provide arts therapists with additional concepts and methods to expand the therapeutic process.

The Safe Place program in Israel is an example of an intervention integrating nature therapy with drama therapy. To date, more than 12,000 kindergarten and schoolchildren in both regular and special-education settings in northern Israel have participated in the Safe Place program. Safe Place is based on the metaphorical relationship between the damage to the forest caused by fires during the second Lebanon war and the forest's recovery. During the program, children are invited to act out their own parallel story within a secure, nature-based setting. They also strengthen their own relationship with nature through such stewardship activities as planting trees and building bird feeders and nesting boxes (Berger, 2020).

Knowing Nature as Healer

Many children suffer from trauma and stress, conditions that can put them at increased risk of mental illness. The healing powers of nature can serve as a buffer in preventing or minimizing the impact of trauma and stress in their lives. While all children should have opportunities to experience the therapeutic benefits of nature engagement, it may be especially important for children with special needs because the impact of a disability on a child's life can be a source of increased stress. It could be that the experience of disability makes engagement with nature "more precious and special to them" (Heintzman, 2014).

SEATTLE'S CHILDREN'S PLAYGARDEN

One way to connect children with special needs with the healing power of nature is through the development of inclusive playgardens. One such place is located in Seattle, where the developers wanted a play space that would tell children, "You belong here. Everyone is welcome." The PlayGarden's website says it well: "At the PlayGarden, children with and without disabilities play, learn, and grow alongside each other. Each child is respected and accepted just the way they are" (Seattle Children's PlayGarden, 2020).

The PlayGarden features different types of gardens and an orchard; a playground with accessible surfacing and play equipment selected to promote inclusion; a variety of animals, such as chickens, ducks, bunnies, a resident cat, therapy dogs, insects, birds, and small woodland animals in their natural habitat; a water feature; an accessible tree fort; a musical sculpture; and plenty of loose parts for open-ended play.

The PlayGarden also offers a nature-based preschool program; approximately half of the children enrolled have special needs. Teachers work closely with families and therapists in accordance with the children's IEPs.

Staff at the PlayGarden have developed several helpful resources on including children with disabilities in community-based settings. You can learn more at https://childrensplaygarden.org

A toolkit for inclusion—one of the resources—includes an extensive glossary of terms specific to the subject of disability and inclusion.

Shiqi Yue, a teacher in a child-care program in Huangshi, China, shared her observations about nature as healer to Dr. Huan Chen:

When Tongtong first came into our nursery, he wasn't following verbal directions or making eye contact with people. According to his parents, until the age of two, Tongtong lived with his grandma, who rarely took him outside of the apartment.

Tongtong was very quiet during his first week in the nursery. He observed his classmates from a corner of the room. We sensed loneliness and helplessness in his eyes, but his response when we reached out to him was to walk away without showing any emotion or direct reaction. So, we gave him space and never pushed him to join any group activity. Gradually, Tongtong developed an emotional connection with his key person, Ms. Fan. Although he barely talked with her, he was willing to hold her hands and seemed to enjoy her caring attention during dining and nap time. However, he was still very reluctant to engage in any other interactions and showed many repetitive behaviors, such as hitting the wall with his head and eating leaves and paper when he was alone. Assessment results indicated that Tongtong had some special educational needs and required intensive intervention.

We established a different schedule for Tongtong and allowed him to go into the outdoor garden when other children were having indoor group activities. He seemed to greatly enjoy his time in the garden. He was much calmer there and sometimes even smiled. He always seemed to have a plan about what he was going to do in the garden. His first exploration involved picking grass and chewing it for a while. He gradually enjoyed other things: running on grass, sitting or lying down under the tree, and crawling through the underground mud tube.

Over the winter, Tongtong developed a special relationship with trees. Every time when we went out of the building, Tongtong would run directly to the big tree in our garden, collect leaves from the ground, and spread them around the roots of the tree. He did not explain to us what he was doing, but we could see happiness on his face and a sparkle in his eyes. Our team discussed this behavior for a long time in our weekly meetings. We believed that Tongtong's leaf collecting was not just a simple repetitive behavior but something with a deeper meaning. We decided to look to the other children for possible clues. We invited them to join Tongtong in his leaf play. We then asked, "Can anybody tell us why you spread leaves under the tree?" One boy answered, "Tongtong is picking up leaves, so we come here to help him." Tongtong seemed relaxed and comfortable with the boy's response. One of the staff commented, "How kind you are to help each other. Should we have a little hug?" It was at that moment that Tongtong accepted the first hug from peers and staff. His key person, Ms. Fan, burst into tears as she witnessed this scene.

Staff continued to ask the children about the leaf collecting: "Does anybody else have different ideas about why you're spreading leaves under the tree?" The children were all busy picking up leaves and ignored this follow-up question. Surprisingly, I heard Tongtong say, "Cold." The children were inspired by Tongtong's answer and started to expand on what he said: "The tree is cold; we are putting cloth on him." "We are making cloth for the tree." "The tree is cold without his fur." Tongtong was smiling during this interaction. We sensed that he was now ready to join the discussion.

We can gather from Tongtong's story that nature provides him with unlimited possibilities to explore and feel, while also embracing him with high tolerance and acceptance. Nature provides so many things beyond what human teachers can offer. Nature teaches through the wind, flowers, plants, birds, clouds . . . Tongtong can chew grass, stomp on the ground, play with mud, and do whatever he wants to do while exploring with his body—and all are accepted. Nature gives Tongtong a place to be away, yet it accompanies him. Tongtong is reluctant to be with peers and adults, but he never refuses nature. He is a part of nature. He feels safe and relaxed when surrounded by nature. Nature's unlimited resources and high

acceptance helped Tongtong gradually feel a sense of belonging in our nursery. He stopped chewing grass and started to notice different features of the natural environment, such as color, shape, and species. Now that he feels comfortable playing freely with the natural world, Tongtong seems ready to open his world to peers, as well.

This chapter focused on ways in which nature can meet some of the emotional needs of young children, including the need to belong, to feel competent and safe, and to experience awe and wonder. The next chapter discusses nature as a play partner and illustrates ways in which engagement with natural materials fosters a young child's imagination and encourages positive peer interactions.

REFERENCES

Arvay, Clemens G. 2018. *The Healing Code of Nature.* Boulder, CO: Sounds True.

Beery, Thomas, Louise Chawla, and Peter Levin. 2020. "Being and Becoming in Nature: Defining and Measuring Connection to Nature in Young Children." *International Journal of Early Childhood Environmental Education* 7(3): 3–22.

Berger, Ronen, and Mooli Lahad. 2013. *The Healing Forest in Post-Crisis Work with Children: A Nature Therapy and Expressive Arts Program for Groups.* London, UK: Jessica Kingsley.

Berger, Ronen. 2020. "Nature Therapy: Incorporating Nature into Arts Therapy." *Journal of Humanistic Psychology* 60(2): 244–257.

Bratman, Gregory N., et al. 2015. "Nature Experience Reduces Rumination and Subgenual Prefrontal Cortex Activation." *PNAS* 112(28): 8567–8572.

Carson, Rachel. 1956. *The Sense of Wonder: A Celebration of Nature for Parents and Children.* New York: HarperCollins.

Chawla, Louise. 1990. "Ecstatic Places." *Children's Environments Quarterly* 7(4): 18–23.

Cooke, Emma, et al. 2020. "'Lie in the Grass, the Soft Grass': Relaxation Accounts of Young Children attending Childcare." *Children and Youth Services Review* 109. doi: http://dx.doi.org/10.1016/j.childyouth.2019.104722

Clinebell, Howard. 1996. *Ecotherapy: Healing Ourselves, Healing the Earth.* New York: Haworth Press.

Crnic, Meghan, and Michelle Kondo. 2019. "Nature Rx: Reemergence of Pediatric Nature-Based Therapeutic Programs from the Late 19th and Early 20th Centuries." *American Journal of Public Health* 109(10): 1371–1378.

Dennis, Jr., Samuel, Christine Kiewra, and Alexandra Wells. 2019. "Natural Outdoor Classrooms: A National Survey Final Report." Dimensions Foundation. https://dimensionsfoundation.org/wp-content/uploads/2019/11/NaturalOutdoorClassrooms_FinalReport_Sept2019.pdf

Engemann, Kristine, et al. 2019. "Residential Green Space in Childhood Is Associated with Lower Risk of Psychiatric Disorders from Adolescence into Adulthood." *PNAS* 116(11): 5188–5193.

Gaminiesfahani, Hedyeh, Mirjana Lozanovska, and Richard Tucker. 2020. "A Scoping Review of the Impact on Children of the Built Environment Design Characteristics of Healing Spaces." *Health Environments Research & Design Journal* 13(4): 98–114.

Hansen, Margaret M., Reo Jones, and Kirsten Tocchini. 2017. "Shinrin-Yoku (Forest Bathing) and Nature Therapy: A State-of-the-Art Review." *International Journal of Environmental Research and Public Health* 14(8): 851. doi: 10.3390/ijerph14080851

Heintzman, Paul. 2014. "Nature-Based Recreation, Spirituality, and Persons with Disabilities." *Journal of Disability and Religion* 18(1): 97–116.

Keller, Helen. 1903/1908. *The World I Live In and Optimism: A Collection of Essays.* New York: Century Co. and T. Y. Crowell and Co.

Kiewra, Christine, and Ellen Veselack. 2016. "Playing with Nature: Supporting Preschoolers' Creativity in Natural Outdoor Classrooms." *The International Journal of Early Childhood Environmental Education* 4(1): 70–95.

La Puma, John. 2019. "Nature Therapy: An Essential Prescription for Health." *Alternative and Complementary Therapies* 25(2): 68–71.

Largo-Wight, Erin, Brian O'Hara, and William Chen. 2016. "The Efficacy of a Brief Nature Sound Intervention on Muscle Tension, Pulse Rate, and Self-Reported Stress: Nature Contact Micro-Break in an Office or Waiting Room." *Health Environments Research and Design Journal* 10(1): 45–51.

McArdle, Karen, Terri Harrison, and Daniel Harrison. 2013. "Does a Nurturing Approach That Uses an Outdoor Play Environment Build Resilience in Children from a Challenging Background?" *Journal of Adventure Education and Outdoor Learning* 13(3): 238–254.

McCormick, Rachel. 2017. "Does Access to Green Space Impact the Mental Well-Being of Children: A Systematic Review." *Journal of Pediatric Nursing* 37(November–December): 3–7.

Mesibov, Gary B., Victoria Shea, and Eric Schopler. 2004. *The TEACCH Approach to Autism Spectrum Disorders*. New York: Springer.

Richardson, Miles. 2019. "Beyond Restoration: Considering Emotion Regulation in Natural Well-Being." *Ecopsychology* 11(2): 123–129.

Richardson, Miles, and David Sheffield. 2017. "Three Good Things in Nature: Noticing Nearby Nature Brings Sustained Increases in Connection with Nature." *Psyecology* 8(1): 1–32.

Roberts, Anna, Joe Hinds, and Paul Camic. 2019. "Nature Activities and Wellbeing in Children and Young People: A Systematic Literature Review." *Journal of Adventure Education and Outdoor Learning* 20(4): 298–318.

Seattle Children's PlayGarden. 2020. Seattle Children's PlayGarden: A Garden for Everyone. https://childrensplaygarden.org/about/

Swank, Jacqueline, et al. 2015. "Initial Investigation of Nature-Based, Child-Centered Play Therapy: A Single-Case Design." *Journal of Counseling and Development* 93(4): 440–450.

Swank, Jacqueline, Kimberly Walker, and Sang Min Shin. 2020. "Indoor Nature-Based Play Therapy: Taking the Natural World Inside the Playroom." *International Journal of Play Therapy* 29(3): 155–162.

Tsunetsugu, Yuko, Bum-Jin Park, and Yoshifumi Miyazaki. 2010. "Trends in Research Related to 'Shinrin-Yoku' (Taking in the Forest Atmosphere or Forest Bathing) in Japan." *Environmental Health and Preventive Medicine* 15(1): 27–37. doi: 10.1007/s12199-009-0091-z

Wilson, Ruth. 2016. *Learning Is in bloom: Cultivating Outdoor Explorations*. Lewisville, NC: Gryphon House.

Yar, Maryam Allah, and Fatemeh Kazemi. 2020. "The Role of Dish Gardens on the Physical and Neuropsychological Improvement of Hospitalized Children." *Urban Forestry and Urban Greening* 53.

CHAPTER 6

Nature as Play Partner

> ❝
>
> It takes time—loose, unstructured dreamtime—
> to experience nature in a meaningful way.
>
> — **RICHARD LOUV**,
> *Last Child in the Woods*

Almost all types of play engage several areas of development simultaneously. Social play, for example, while promoting such social skills as sharing, cooperating, and negotiating, also promotes language and other forms of self-expression. Dramatic play promotes imagination and creativity as well as mental and emotional competence. Many forms of play help children regulate their emotional states, including feelings of anxiety and aggression. Children generally experience joy and happiness as they play. Such experiences contribute to mental health and quality of life. Play helps children develop a sense of self, as they learn about who they are in relation to the world around them. Through play, children also develop a sense of independence and feelings of self-worth.

Unstructured play is crucial for children's development, and the benefits of play are universal for all children, including children with special needs. Children learn as they play, but play also helps them learn how to learn. We simply need to watch children as they play in nature to see problem solving in action. A child trying to walk across a slippery log needs to figure out how to stay balanced while accomplishing this feat, all the while developing strength, agility, gross-motor control, and physical confidence.

Nature invites authentic play—a form of play that is open ended and freely chosen—the best kind of play for young children. The natural environment matches well with what young children want and need. We might call this a "goodness of fit," in that young children and nature make good play partners.

In this chapter about nature as play partner, we'll look at what the research has to say about the benefits of play, especially play in outdoor environments. We'll also consider the special benefits of nature play for children with differing abilities and ways in which playspaces can be more inclusive.

Benefits of Play

The benefits of play—whether indoors or outdoors—are cumulative; the skills, knowledge, and emotional gains developed through play have both short- and long-term effects on children's development. Neuroscience research suggests that play activity may actually help sculpt the brain, which may explain why play is most prevalent during childhood, the most consequential period of brain development. One thing we know from research is that the frontal lobes of the brain begin developing in early childhood and do not complete until after age twenty-one. As John Medina (2014) explains in *Brain Rules*, functions of the frontal lobe involve skills associated with executive functioning: problem solving, maintaining attention, decision making, and inhibiting emotional impulses. Children need robust executive-functioning skills to do well socially, emotionally, and academically.

Researcher Victoria Carr and colleagues (2017) found that children's play with natural materials, such as logs and tree cookies, in natural playscapes is especially effective in promoting executive functioning in young children. The researchers found evidence of children setting their own goals, solving problems, focusing attention, demonstrating cognitive flexibility, as well as showing inhibitory control, initiation, flexibility, working memory, planning and organization, and monitoring. Another study (Faber Taylor and Butts-Wilmsmeyer, 2020) conducted with kindergarten children in Canada found a positive link between children's self-regulation and time spent playing outdoors in green schoolyards. This study showed that the more often, and the more minutes weekly, that children visited green schoolyards, the greater the gains in self-regulation.

Nature Play

As children dig in the sand, bury themselves in a pile of leaves, and "paint" with mud, they're engaged in a form of play referred to as *nature play*. Children are using the affordances—or gifts—of the natural environment to play. Nature play isn't just any form of outdoor play; it involves playing *with* nature, not just *in* nature. Shooting baskets on an outdoor court, for example, would not be nature play. The basketball court is a built environment, and the basketball a manufactured material. While there are many benefits associated with shooting baskets, nature play offers different types of benefits.

Play with natural materials indoors is a great way to engage children in manipulating and exploring, which encourage fine-motor, language and vocabulary, and social development. While teachers often place natural materials in the science center, natural materials shouldn't be limited to that center—they should be placed throughout the room. Sandra Duncan and Jody Martin, in *Bringing the Outside In* (2018), encourage the infusion of nature in all areas and on all surfaces. They provide multiple examples of how adding nature and natural materials to walls, ceilings, shelves, tabletops, and even the floor of an indoor environment can enrich all areas of learning and invite more imaginative play. For example, children can decorate a branch attached to a wall with ribbons, beads, drawings, and twigs or may even try building a nest with grass and mud, and placing it on a branch. Wooden shadow boxes on the wall invite manipulative and imaginary play. Shadow boxes with compartments are great for playing with small natural materials, such as stones, shells, or pinecones.

Children play differently in outdoor natural environments than they do indoors or on traditional playgrounds. Research on the play behaviors of young children (Kuh, Ponte, and Chau, 2013) shows that play tends to be more complex in outdoor natural environments than in other settings. Play in nature also tends to be more cooperative and play episodes are sustained over longer periods of time than in other settings.

Nature as Play Partner

Nature can be much more than a setting or something to use—it can be a play partner.

Recent research supports this idea. Goodenough, Waite, and Wright (2020) studied children's play on an adventure playground located in a wooded area, observed the transactions between trees and children, and recorded both environmental and human effects. The children frequently used trees, sticks, and plants for imaginary play and social interactions. At times, children's play activities visibly affected the trees and other plants, yet such use seemed to be in response to the "plants' invitations." The trees, for example, "appeared to invite young players to climb and enjoy the sensations accompanying being raised up." This play suggested a partnership between children and the other-than-human environment—a partnership that gave children "valued opportunities to change their emotional mood and trees, to grow." Both the children and the environment were active participants in the process, and both were mutually transformed.

Educators also have noted the relationship of nature as a play partner as they observe children in the natural world. Xi Yang and Meixi Yan are teachers in a program for children with special needs at the Dali Yuanshan Academy in Dali, Yunnan Province, China. The teachers shared these observations about one of their students, Songsong, with Dr. Huan Chen:

> Songsong joined our nursery when he was four years old. At the time, he was not eating independently, could not speak, and didn't want to interact with peers. He was physically strong but showed very unstable emotions. He generally rejected any hugs to calm him down.
>
> Soon after he joined us, we noticed that what he liked the most was going outside. Our kindergarten has a big natural outdoor area. Songsong spent hours running around the grass. He was not kind to our plants, however, constantly snapping off leaves or stomping on grass with all his strength. Many of our plants did not survive Songsong's aggressive behavior. At one point, he spent almost the entire day kicking a little bamboo plant. He just kept kicking and stomping on it. Songsong tended to do the same with plants when we took him out to a wider field. He could focus for two hours on running and kicking until he could see the soil. If water was nearby, Songsong would add water to the mud and engage in messy play. On several occasions, his parents found him fully covered by mud!
>
> Songsong also liked to play in the pond. He could walk in and play with the water the entire day—sometimes with shoes on, sometimes without. It was hard for Songsong to spend any length of time indoors. We often had a staff member take him out for a long walk during the day. We have large farming fields around our nursery where Songsong loved to follow the dirt paths hidden among the crops. Walking through freshly plowed fields helped Songsong develop motor coordination and balance skills. The uneven surface forced him to use his arms to help with balancing. At times, he even crawled, which helped his sensory-processing ability as well.

Songsong was reluctant to play with sand when he first came to the nursery. After many times of walking and crawling in the field, he got used to the uncomfortable feeling under his feet and could then enjoy sand play. This opened a path for him to join his peers in play, as sand is always the most popular area in our kindergarten. We soon saw Songsong walking around children who were playing with sand. The children didn't really want to invite him into their play because they didn't understand his language. Some children, however, gave him high-fives when they achieved a little goal in their sand play. That made him happy. Now after two years in our kindergarten, Songsong can actually play with his peers in some way.

Even though Songsong hasn't always been kind to nature, nature seems to be Songsong's best friend. He seems more relaxed when he's in nature. All his peers are fluent in spoken language, and that gives him enormous hidden pressure. But since nature doesn't use spoken language, that source of pressure is gone. Songsong never shows strong negative emotions when he's in nature. He and nature seem to have a language that only the two of them can understand. Perhaps the higher amount of physical movement in nature also helps.

Nature seems to be Songsong's guide and mentor. We notice that when he's outside Songsong is calmer and seems more motivated to express himself. He's constantly exploring the environment around him and wants to share his findings with us.

Play for Children with Special Needs

Typically developing children readily engage in various forms of both solitary and social play. They find play pleasurable, need little guidance or support on how to play, and learn how to play by playing with peers and by using a variety of materials.

Playing and learning how to play can be more difficult for children with special needs. Certain delays and impairments, such as those in language, speech, and communication, can impede the process. This is not surprising, as these areas of development often occur along with other forms of disability, including autism, hearing impairments, and visual impairments. There are other reasons, too, why children with special needs tend to remain socially isolated during play. Children with physical disabilities may have restricted mobility. Children with cognitive delays may not understand the complexity of play scenarios. Children with socio-emotional challenges may have difficulty initiating and/or maintaining appropriate social interactions.

The environment also influences children's social play behaviors. Some environments encourage more social inclusion than others. Flexible settings and materials are facilitators; they encourage inclusion. For example, open-ended settings with loose movable parts offer more flexibility and inclusion than traditional playgrounds. Typical playgrounds generally consist of playground equipment and open space, which encourage large-muscle activity and offer children limited ways of moving and interacting with their world. Natural environments that include natural loose parts, on the other hand, encourage all types of play, including construction and dramatic play.

Natural loose parts, such as stones, leaves, and pinecones, are materials that children can manipulate and use in different ways. Adding some manufactured tools and materials can extend children's play and learning with natural loose parts. Shovels and buckets in the sandbox or dirt pile, for example, encourage digging and pouring. A variety of kitchen utensils promotes children's dramatic play with plant parts and water. Large cardboard boxes can be used for den building; small boxes for collecting, carrying, and sorting. Observation tools, such as hand lenses and binoculars, can encourage children to look more closely at the natural world around them. Measurement tools, compasses, bug-collecting boxes, and field guides can also invite closer observation.

Some loose parts invite children to get wet or dirty, but some children (and/or families) may not be comfortable with this. Providing towels for wet hands and a bucket of water for dirty feet can ease these concerns. Long-handled tools and working gloves can also be helpful for some children who may not want to get their hands dirty.

Natural loose materials have all the features needed for more inclusive play. Children of varying needs, abilities, and backgrounds can use the materials in a variety of ways without making mistakes or wondering if what they're doing is the right way to do it. There is no "right way" to dig a hole in the sand or make a nature collage. For an observant teacher or therapist, natural materials can also serve as assessment tools, especially for children with limited speech and language skills. A child may not be able to tell you that sand is heavier than leaves, but watch a child closely and you may

RESEARCH NOTE
AFFORDANCES OF THE WOODS

Researchers Louise Chawla and colleagues collected information about how children with language-based learning disabilities used and experienced the outdoor areas at their school (Chawla et al., 2014). The outdoor areas consisted of an athletic field, a built playground, and two acres of woods. During afternoon recess and after-school programs, children were free to choose where they wanted to play.

During three fall seasons, 96 percent of the students chose the woods as their regular recess location. While there, the children often played with "sticks, rocks, water, dirt, fruit, leaves, and other found objects in creative ways." They also hunted for frogs, salamanders, and other small animals. Play for the six- and seven-year-old children consisted primarily of exploratory and sensory-based activities, such as wading, splashing, digging, and smashing rocks. Play for the eight- to ten-year-old children tended to consist of activities "within a fort culture that involved role-playing and other imaginative processes such as crafting shelters, tools, and play structures."

In analyzing the data, the researchers found that the woods promoted cooperative alliances, autonomy, and competence. The younger children worked together as they negotiated the uneven terrain of the hillside and creek bed. They encouraged each other to explore new places and sensations. One of the eight-year-olds commented on how fort building and related play gave him a sense of power and that he enjoyed the freedom and independence he experienced in the woods. He also noted how playing in the woods was "definitely a good way to make friends."

A mother of an extremely dyslexic student observed that, while so much is generally hard for her daughter, being in the woods wasn't hard and that it leveled the playing field for her. She noted how the woods provided "a safe place to test out different roles." Another mother described the woods as a "safe haven" for her son socially. "When the woods closed for the winter, his anxiety rose."

Most of the students who participated in this study had transferred to the school after attending other schools or programs. The researchers were thus able to draw comparisons between the different school experiences. When asked, "How did recess at your previous school compare to the recesses you have now?" all of the participating students expressed negative feelings about recess at their previous schools. One child described it as torture: "'Cause there was nothing to do." In contrast, they described recess at their current school as a positive and stress-free experience. In the new environment, they felt, as one child exclaimed, "Happy! Really, really happy!" Another child said, "I can just be myself there!"

see that he has figured it out. He might fill a bucket with leaves and carry it across the yard, but then put only a small amount of sand in the bucket when he wants to add sand to the leaf pile.

In addition to the myriad of natural loose parts, other features of a natural environment encourage children's play: trees invite climbing, hills encourage sledding, and secluded places inspire hiding or resting. Wooded places, in particular, are often favorite places to play, and there's research to back up the idea that natural schoolyards can reduce children's stress and promote resilience, especially for children with special needs.

Helen McDonald, pedagogical director of the Collaborative Teachers Institute in Santa Fe, New Mexico, shared this experience about how the open-endedness of a sandbox allowed young children to enter into an imaginary world where they are free to confront some challenging issues in their lives:

> Teachers at this preschool noticed an emotional intensity building in the classroom of fourteen children ranging in age from three to five. The teachers were aware that some of the families were in crisis. The father of one child with ADHD was battling alcoholism. A child had a parent dealing with drug addiction and domestic abuse. Another child had a teen mother who was facing some difficult challenges. A child had parents in the process of getting a divorce. In hopes of helping the children, the teachers started adding extra supports beyond access to the usual arts- and play-based curriculum.
>
> One day, several children got very interested in digging in the sandbox. They went back to this activity the next day, and several other children joined them. This activity continued for at least a week. The teachers provided more shovels, flashlights, goggles, measuring tape, and other tools as the children requested them. The children explained to the teachers that they were going to leave their parents and teachers and go live underground in their "Adventure Hole." Each day at clean-up time, the children, with the help of a teacher, carefully covered the hole to protect it. The children were determined to continue their work the next day.
>
> While this play scenario demonstrates children's interest in having an adventure in nature, it also demonstrates their efforts to make a world of their own. As the following dialogue illustrates, the children were working together to create a place where they could feel safe and take care of each other. The children seemed to be therapeutically choosing to lean into a rich game of imagining adventures in nature. This form of play gave children a taste of freedom and the possibility of redefining themselves.
>
> TANISHA: We are digging the biggesy hole ever—it's an adventure hole! We're making it so big, so we can all get in!
>
> TEACHER: Robbie just asked me why you are digging that hole.
>
> TANISHA: We're going to live underground. We will drink water and juice and eat a little bit of sugar and a lot of strong food. But if we found a garden underground, we could just eat from it.

MICHAEL: Do I need a weapon down there?

TANISHA: Don't worry! We will be fine down there! Only kids will live there. It won't be cold down there—we will be protected from the sun and rain! We will have fun, fun, fun, and no one else! We will eat worms and crickets, grasshoppers, and a little bit of sugar and juice.

The Inclusive Playspace

The Individuals with Disabilities Education Act (IDEA) mandates educating children with disabilities in public schools in the least restrictive environment. This law was established, in part, to ensure that children with special needs would have the opportunity to interact with their typically developing peers. Some research, however, indicates that children with disabilities (Hestenes and Carroll, 2000) may be socially isolated in inclusive classrooms and that typically developing children are more likely to interact with their typically developing peers than with their peers with special needs. Access to the regular classroom, then, doesn't always equate to inclusion in instructional and social activities. A child with special needs may be present in the classroom—and perhaps even occupied with materials—but still not socially engaged.

A well-designed inclusive playspace reduces barriers for children with special needs, creating an environment where children with differing abilities can engage in similar play behaviors with their typically developing peers. Hopefully, this will also lead to socially inclusive play—that is, where children with and without special needs play together. There are some indications that this is more likely to occur outdoors rather than indoors (Price, 2019). The opportunities for and benefits of inclusion, then, for children with special needs may be greater outdoors than indoors.

An *inclusive playground* can be defined as a playspace designed to reduce barriers for children with disabilities, creating an environment where children with special needs can engage in similar play behaviors with their typically developing peers. Nicholas LeSchofs (2020) looked at what types of outdoor playspaces encouraged the most dramatic play among first and second graders with and without disabilities. The study also examined whether a well-designed inclusive playground would reduce the differences between play behaviors of children with and without disabilities.

LeSchofs and colleagues observed eighty-nine children (more than half with special needs) at an inclusive playground at Edith Bowen Laboratory School in Utah. The playground included nature-play areas landscaped with numerous accommodations to support play, such as stage-like areas, natural props, enclosed areas, slightly themed settings, and open-ended settings, which offered children opportunities for dramatic play. The settings where the children were free to manipulate the materials in the environment as they desired invited the most dramatic play. The least amount of dramatic play occurred in static or stationary settings or settings with only one main purpose. Researchers noted a small difference in the dramatic-play types among children with and without disabilities. In fact, the children with disabilities participated in all types of play on the playground, even though some interactions were not at the same level as the children without disabilities. The fact that some playspaces are purposefully designed or adapted to be accessible for children with disabilities doesn't guarantee that those who use them will experience these spaces as positive, inclusive, or enjoyable. Observations of different playspaces reveal a general absence of families with children with special needs. One community in Colorado addressed this concern by inviting children to share their ideas about how to make playspaces more inclusive and friendlier for all children.

A group of seven- and eight-year-old children participated in the Growing Up Boulder project (Hill and Chawla, 2019) to share ideas about how to make playgrounds accessible and attractive to children with special needs. Work for this project focused on Universal Access Design (UAD), a system of design strategies for making indoor and outdoor spaces accessible for people of all abilities. After learning about the concept of UAD, the children responded to the following questions relating to playground design from researchers:

- ❁ What do you want a playground to have?
- ❁ What do you need from a playground?
- ❁ What should a playground have so that everyone can play?
- ❁ Do you believe UAD is an important concept to incorporate in playground design?

Once the children understood UAD and its purpose, they decided that a playground where everyone can play should be "safe," "fun," "novel," and "inclusive" for children of all abilities. They identified four main categories of features such a playground should have:

1. Quiet spaces where children with sensory processing disorder can find a quiet refuge to relax
2. Nature where all children can engage in nature play and feel nature's relaxing and calming properties
3. Accommodating structures that can provide fun and safe play for children of all abilities
4. Accommodating textures that promote mobility for children of all abilities

They felt that inclusive playgrounds should also include trees, open green spaces, flowers, tree trunks, a tree house, and rocks.

This chapter discussed the importance of play to child development and described ways in which natural environments and natural materials can enhance the play experience for children with differing abilities. Chapter 7 highlights ways in which nature engagement and nature connectedness can promote some often-overlooked aspects of child development, including the ecological self and spiritual development.

REFERENCES

Carr, Victoria, et al. 2017. "Nature by Design: Playscape Affordances Support the Use of Executive Function in Preschoolers." *Children, Youth and Environments* 27(2): 25–46.

Chawla, Louise, et al. 2014. "Green Schoolyards as Havens from Stress and Resources for Resilience in Childhood and Adolescence." *Health and Place* 28: 1–13.

Duncan, Sandra, and Jody Martin. 2018. *Bringing the Outside In: Ideas for Creating Nature-Based Classroom Experiences for Young Children*. Lincoln, NE: Exchange Press.

Faber Taylor, Andrea, and Carrie Butts-Wilmsmeyer. 2020. "Self-Regulation Gains in Kindergarten Related to Frequency of Green Schoolyard Use." *Journal of Environmental Psychology* 70.

Goodenough, Alice, Sue Waite, and Nick Wright. 2020. "Place as Partner: Material and Affective Intra-Play between Young People and Trees." *Children's Geographies* 19(2): 225–240.

Hestenes, Linda L., and Deborah Carroll. 2000. "The Play Interactions of Young Children With and Without Disabilities: Individual and Environmental Influences." *Early Childhood Research Quarterly* 15(2): 229–246.

Hill, Catherine, and Louise Chawla. 2019. "Fun, Novel, Safe, and Inclusive: Children's Design Recommendations for Playgrounds for All Abilities." *Children, Youth and Environments* 29(1): 105–115.

Kuh, Lisa, Iris Ponte, and Clement Chau. 2013. "The Impact of a Natural Playscape Installation on Young Children's Play Behaviors." *Children, Youth and Environments* 23(2): 49–77.

LeSchofs, Nicholas R. 2020. "Dramatic Play Affordances of Outdoor Settings for First and Second Grade Children with and without Disabilities." Digital Commons, Utah State University. https://digitalcommons.usu.edu/etd/7769/

Loebach, Janet, and Adina Cox. 2020. "Tool for Observing Play Outdoors (TOPO): A New Typology for Capturing Children's Play Behaviors in Outdoor Environments." *International Journal of Environmental Research and Public Health* 17(15): 5611.

Medina, John. 2014. *Brain Rules: 12 Principles for Surviving and Thriving at Work, Home, and School*. Seattle, WA: Pear Press.

Price, Alan. 2019. "Using Outdoor Learning to Augment Social and Emotional Learning (SEL) Skills in Young People with Social, Emotional, and Behavioural Difficulties (SEBD)." *Journal of Adventure Education and Outdoor Learning* 19(4): 315–328.

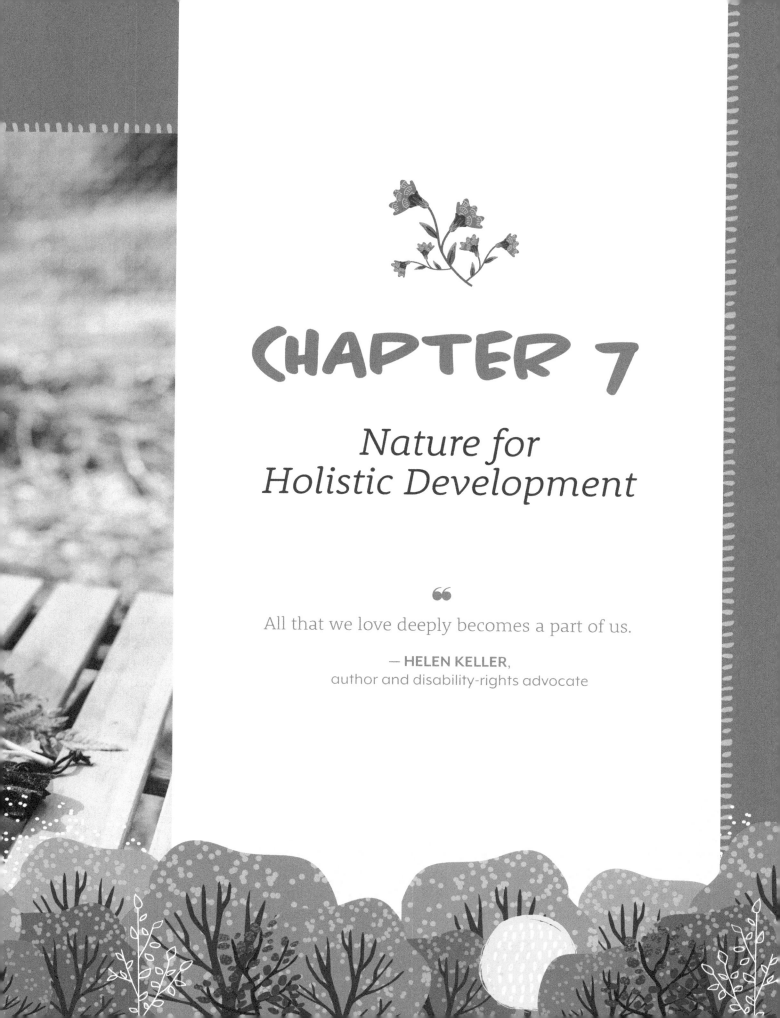

CHAPTER 7

Nature for Holistic Development

"

All that we love deeply becomes a part of us.

— **HELEN KELLER,**
author and disability-rights advocate

While many early childhood programs use the term *holistic development* in their descriptions and mission statements, its meaning isn't always well understood. Holistic development generally refers to a philosophy or belief system that considers the whole child and her environment. This philosophy recognizes that internal and external factors influence how a child develops during the early years as well as the multidimensional aspects of child development.

External factors influencing the holistic development of the young child include the physical environment, social and cultural experiences, and attitudes and beliefs of families and caregivers. Some external factors, such as poverty, neglect, and abuse, can impede the development of a child. Other factors—such as general health, disposition, and personal interests—are internal to the child.

If a child has a disability, that, too, will affect his or her development. A holistic approach in working with young children, however, will focus on the child, not the disability. As Tiffany Yu, the founder and CEO of Diversability, reminds us, "People with disabilities are more than just 'people with disabilities.' . . . [They] are people with diverse abilities."

A holistic approach focuses on these abilities and on the environments in which the young child lives, plays, and learns. The process involves viewing each child as a whole person—physically, intellectually, emotionally, socially, culturally, and spiritually—and providing environments that promote growth in each of these areas. This chapter focuses on ways in which natural environments and a child's connectedness to nature play a role in this process.

※
Connectedness to Nature

Connectedness to nature refers to an individual's subjective sense of her relationship with the natural world. This form of connectedness means more than physical connecting with nature; it includes cognitive, emotional, and experiential components. People vary along a continuum in their connection to nature. For some people, the connection is very strong; for others, somewhat less influential. While nature connectedness tends to be relatively stable across time and situations, a person's subjective connection to nature can fluctuate with different situations and can deepen over time.

People who feel strongly connected to nature tend to differ in some ways from people who do not (Nisbet, Zelenski, and Murphy, 2008). High connectedness is generally associated with personality traits such as conscientious and openness. People who feel strongly connected to nature tend to spend more time outdoors and show a greater willingness to engage in sustainable actions. Connectedness to nature is also linked to emotional, psychological, and spiritual well-being.

Nature relatedness, sometimes referred to as *nature connectedness*, is a basic psychological human need (Baxter and Pelletier, 2018) and has a positive effect on human health, especially in the areas of the way the body functions, psychological well-being, and cognitive recovery from *attentional fatigue*—a decreased ability to concentrate. Related research with children shows that nature near the home, knowledge about the environment, and previous experience in nature are positively linked to children's connection to nature (Cheng and Monroe, 2012). This research also indicates that children's connectedness to nature tends to be reflected in enjoyment of nature, empathy for creatures, a sense of oneness, and a sense of responsibility. Other research found some interesting links between children's connectedness to nature and certain emotional and behavioral attributes (Sobko, Jia, and Brown, 2018):

✿ Children who enjoyed nature showed less distress.

✿ Children who showed greater responsibility toward nature tended to be less hyperactive and had fewer behavioral and peer difficulties.

✿ Children who showed a greater awareness of nature displayed fewer emotional difficulties.

Another research study (Bakir-Demir, Berument, and Sahin-Acar, 2019) explored how the level of nature connectedness affects the relationship between having greenery nearby and children's regulation skills. The researchers studied the link between greenery around children's homes and three areas of self-regulation: cognitive, emotional, and behavioral. Researchers found that children living in areas with more greenery reported higher levels of nature connectedness. As levels of nature connectedness increased, so did the children's cognitive and emotional regulation skills.

There are many reasons, then, to look to nature as a resource in promoting children's holistic development. Ideas for doing this are outlined in different sections of this book, and there are many other resources available through such professional organizations as the Natural Start Alliance (www.naturalstart.org), the Children & Nature Network (www.childrenandnature.org), Nature Explore (www.natureexplore.org), and the Natural Learning Initiative (https://design.ncsu. edu/research/natural-learning-initiative/). Many of these resources reflect an understanding that there are different pathways to connectedness to nature. Researchers from the University of Derby (Lumber, Richardson, and Sheffield, 2018) identified seven such pathways:

✿ Investigating nature through scientific inquiry

✿ Engaging the senses

✿ Creating idyllic nature, or nature consistent with individual preferences

✿ Noting nature through artistry, such as photography or painting

✿ Nature conservation

✿ Growing food

✿ Engaging with wild nature, such as nondomesticated animals or natural rather than built environments

All of these pathways can be made available to young children, including children with differing abilities.

Ecological Self

Connectedness to nature overlaps in some ways with an understanding of the ecological self—also referred to as *ecological identity*. Ecological self refers to an individual's connection with and attitudes toward the natural environment, which is a part of a child's holistic development. A healthy ecological self includes such positive environmental values as appreciating and caring for the natural world and can expand and mature over time. Different factors influence how a child's ecological self will develop, including where the child lives and plays, cultural values and experiences, and educational experiences. Perhaps the most influential factor in the development of a healthy ecological self during childhood is the opportunity for frequent, positive experiences in and with the natural world.

Carie Green, an associate professor and endowed director of early childhood education and outreach at South Dakota State University, has conducted research on the development of children's environmental identity (Green, Kalvaitis, and Worster, 2016; Green, 2016; Green, 2017; Green, 2018). She has learned that children perceive and act upon the natural world in their own unique ways. In the following contribution, Green explains that how children understand and interact with nature depends on past and present experiences, interactions with peers and adults, and their own agency. As part of her research, she has used wearable cameras positioned on children's foreheads to get a child's-eye view of children's experiences as they play and explore (Green, 2016). In reviewing children's micro-interactions with their environments, she has identified four stages of environmental identity development. She has also found ways that educators can support children in developing a healthy environmental identity.

- **Trust in nature versus mistrust in nature:** Trust in nature forms the foundation of children developing a strong bond with their environment. If children are unable to work through their feelings of anxiety and uncertainty during outdoor explorations, then they may choose to avoid the environment altogether. It is important that educators and other adults provide consistent opportunities for children to interact with the environment in a safe and secure way. This might mean patiently encouraging a child to observe and develop a sense of wonder for natural phenomena. It is also important that children be clothed properly while outside; physical discomfort might discourage further environmental exploration.

- **Spatial autonomy versus environmental shame:** As children develop comfort in their environments, they are more likely to venture out on their own or with others to explore, develop skills, and make connections with their environment. However, in developing this sense of spatial autonomy, children may experience feelings of environmental shame, a loss of confidence and/or frustration in their abilities. They may waver between feeling confident and feeling inadequate in their abilities to navigate their environment. For example, if a child attempts to climb a tree and struggles, ultimately losing confidence and falling to the ground, the child might not think he or she is able to climb a tree—something many children are interested in doing. An adult might ask children how comfortable they feel in climbing and what they want to learn, encouraging them with the advice that new skills take time and practice. Specifically, a supportive adult might encourage children to carefully consider the placement of their hands and feet on stable branches and might advise children to test the limits of a branch before fully placing their weight on it. The adult might also prompt to gauge how safe they feel as they ascend a tree. By providing an opportunity for self-reflection, educators can support children in developing confidence in their abilities.

• **Environmental competency versus environmental disdain:** Environmental competency entails not only ecological understanding of the environment but also the way a person emotionally and behaviorally interacts with it. Emotions can range from excitement to confidence to uncertainty and disregard. For example, consider a group of children who decide to climb a tree, imagining that a monster is coming. One child is enthusiastic and climbs easily; she calls the tree a "secret tree." Another child is quite nervous and unsure, calling the tree "stupid." The first child begins to use that language too, calling the tree "stupid" even as she continues to climb. She initially claimed the tree as a secret space, gaining a sense of spatial autonomy. She climbed the tree easily, demonstrating that her environmental competency is more advanced than her peer's. She remained enthusiastic about climbing in the face of her peer's worry and doubt, but she adopts the language of disdain. Peers can influence the perception of another living being and, if not redirected, may over time create a *sense of environmental disdain*, disregard for another living being. Adults can influence children in the development of empathy. They can teach children that a tree is another living being and, like humans, needs water and nutrients for survival and benefits from love and care. An adult might point out ways that humans care for trees by planting them in the right place, mulching, pruning, and watering young trees in the first few years. The adult could also point out the many benefits that trees provide for humans if they are properly cared for.

• **Environmental action versus environmental harm:** Children's progression through the first three stages of environmental identity development will ultimately lead them to engage in environmental action or environmental harm. While acts of care and stewardship will result from the development of healthy environmental competency, harm (whether intentional or unintentional) might result from improperly developed environmental competency and/or environmental disdain. Guided education for the environment is so important. It is not enough just to send children outdoors for free play and exploration, although this certainly has its benefit. What we do not want in our zealous quest to get children outdoors is to endorse behaviors that, if not corrected and redirected, will lead to a hardening of the human-nature binary that endorses dominion and control. Through their play, children may experience nature as an object to be mastered and controlled. Their actions may then devalue a plant or animal as a living and breathing organism. Adult involvement in children's play activities to some extent could help prevent incidents of environmental harm.

We need to critically consider what types of nature experiences we are encouraging and endorsing and nurture a strong sense of belonging where children recognize themselves as a part of nature and nature as a part of them. Each child's path of environmental identity development is unique, dynamic, fluid, and constantly evolving. Weaknesses should not be seen as shortcomings but opportunities for nurturing growth. Intentional educational strategies can be used to support children in the development of environmental competencies and dispositions of care and stewardship of other living beings.

While the ecological self is a part of who we are, it's often overlooked in efforts to promote the holistic development of young children. This may relate to the misunderstanding that fostering the development of the ecological self is more about "saving the Earth" than promoting child development. In reality, it's about both. Without a healthy relationship with nature, children are missing an important part of their development. A healthy ecological self expands a child's circle of concern as the child matures from an *ego*centric view of the world to a more *eco*centric view. This shift is good for the child and good for the Earth.

A child's connectedness to nature and the development of his or her ecological self are closely intertwined. Promoting one promotes the other. Both contribute to a child's quality of life and a sense of well-being. The well-being benefits gained from childhood engagement with nature tend to remain with the individual as she grows into adulthood. People who have been physically and emotionally close to nature during childhood are likely to carry with them into adulthood an ecological sense of well-being that acknowledges kinship and interdependence with other living creatures and the rest of the natural world. This sense of kinship and interdependence is an important contributor to a person's quality of life.

Holistic development in partnership with the natural world is best accomplished through open-ended active play. Young children need the freedom to actively explore the environment and to test their abilities. The freedom to follow their own interests and to check things out through trial and error builds self-esteem and self-confidence. An understanding of self and of self in relation to the natural world aren't understandings that are "given" to a child. Such understandings need to be constructed. Children construct understandings—or develop concepts—through repeated interactions with the physical and social entities of the world in which they live.

In the following reflection, Nancy Rosenow, author of *Heart-Centered Teaching Inspired by Nature*, discusses how nature-based teaching and learning contribute to the holistic development of teachers as well as children.

As my journey to bring richer and deeper connections with nature to children has grown over the years, I've realized that educators and families benefit as much as children. My book was written in an attempt to encourage adults to discover how much nature connections can support them in their work.

An extensive research study carried out with multiple sites over a number of years documented that educators who teach in nature-based outdoor classrooms report positive personal benefits. An excerpt from the study states that most educators with access to these spaces reported that they "felt refreshed and patient and therefore better able to respond to children's needs; they felt increased effectiveness in their work as they were able to adjust activities to the appropriate level for children and more able to calm upset children" (Dennis, Kiewra, and Wells, 2019).

I remember visiting a teacher in the Los Angeles Unified School District, which has made a commitment to getting natural outdoor classrooms into all their early education centers. She told me what a difference the new nature-based space made for her. "It's allowed me to be the kind of educator I always knew I could be." I've heard this kind of comment from educators throughout the United States and Canada, and because of our collaboration with the World Forum Foundation on Early Care and Education, from all parts of the globe.

My commitment to heart-centered teaching inspired by nature comes from my belief in a way of supporting children from a place of love for each other and a place of awe and appreciation for the wonders of the world around us. I believe that nature can help us—adult and child alike—discover who we are on the most authentic level, and what we each can uniquely contribute to making our world a better place.

Nature and a Sense of Well-Being

Well-being enables us to function well in different dimensions of our lives: psychologically, physically, emotionally, socially, and spiritually. Well-being can take many forms, but it generally means feeling good, functioning well, feeling happy, and having a sense of purpose or meaning in life. As explained in earlier chapters, nature connectedness and well-being are positively linked, particularly in the areas of emotional, psychological, and spiritual well-being.

The understanding that both exposure to and connection with nature can contribute to a sense of well-being is based on an impressive body of research. The focus of much of this research, however, has been on short-term physiological and psychological mood states rather than longer-term well-being (Pritchard et al., 2019). Some studies have identified several pathways (Cleary et al., 2017) through which nature promotes a type of well-being called *eudaimonic well-being*, well-being that includes self-realization and living life in a full and purposeful way, over a longer term. Having access to therapeutic natural landscapes on a regular basis is one such pathway.

Until recently, the idea of therapeutic landscapes was generally associated with healing gardens that were part of hospitals or other health-care settings. This concept now recognizes the potential healing effects of everyday landscapes, such as the home environment, community gardens, urban public parks, and sensory gardens. Sensory gardens appeal to all the senses and promote a feeling of being fully immersed in the natural world. A well-designed sensory garden transports the user to a "place away"—a world apart from the sights, sounds, and smells of the built environment.

Time in nature—especially in the form of unstructured, less supervised, and risky play—allows children to develop a sense of confidence in their own abilities and in their risk assessments of what is safe and what is not (Cleary et al., 2017). This sense of self-efficacy helps individuals benefit from everyday therapeutic landscapes into adulthood.

Marisa, Sierra's mother, described to me how time in nature has helped her daughter develop a sense of confidence.

> Sierra is an eleven-year-old who is deafblind. She loves nature and has been working as a nature advocate for the past four years. Her primary focus is on climate activism. She's been working with Global WE, a youth climate activism organization, for the last four years and is now on their board. Marisa describes her as "bright, fierce, passionate, and resourceful" and as someone who is "deeply passionate when it comes to caring about all the living things in our world."
>
> As an activist, Sierra has given presentations at the capitol building in Santa Fe, New Mexico, spoken with land and resources lawyers at public meetings, and been involved with climate strikes at school.
>
> When asked what nature means to her, Sierra explains through an interpreter, "Nature is all around us, part of us, and it is our home." Sierra also talks about nature in the context of love. "Nature is love and provides us with love and care." Some of Sierra's favorite natural places are up in the mountains and near creeks, rivers, and lakes. She loves the delicious smell of warm pine forests and any place with dirt.
>
> Sierra explains that, while she has vision and hearing challenges, she can feel a lot in nature: "breathing in the fresh air, feeling the earth between my toes." Nature for Sierra is beautiful and calming. "It helps lessen my stress. It helps me feel connected. It also helps me think of new things. Being in a favorite natural place in nature helps me feel more comfortable and even more adventurous."
>
> Marisa explains that Sierra has been outside during much of her life, in all seasons. She also notes how time in nature offers challenges and opportunities for children like Sierra: "Their other senses are strong and heightened [and] nature offers plenty of things to feel. It also offers various challenges to work through. This helps with creativity and problem solving."
>
> Sierra doesn't always enjoy hiking due to balance and vision needs, so the family compromises by taking more accessible hikes or staying near camping areas. Sierra enjoys responsibilities such as gathering wood, starting fires, cooking over a fire, helping set up shelter, and babysitting her younger brother.

Sierra's art

In addition to being Sierra's mom, Marisa is also the director of a forest school program that serves young children with various disabilities. She encourages educators and other adults working with children with special needs to meet them where they are, make sure they're comfortable, and then go from there. Marisa highlights the importance of outdoor time, which she notes doesn't need to be structured because "all the little moments mean a lot."

Nature and Spiritual Development

Until recently, much of the literature on the link between nature-based experiences and spirituality has been conceptual and speculative. This is changing. Research recognizes spiritual health as one of the dimensions of holistic health (Hawks, 1994). In his review of the research, Paul Heintzman supports the understanding that nature-related experiences can provide both short- and long-term spiritual health benefits (Heintzman, 2014). He suggests that the spiritual health benefits of nature engagement may be especially effective for persons with disabilities and that such benefits can play an important role in their holistic development.

Deb Schein, author of *Inspiring Wonder, Awe, and Empathy: Spiritual Development for Children*, also recognizes spirituality as an integral component of holistic health. She, too, considers nature engagement to be a powerful resource for promoting spiritual development. Schein notes that young children's first response to nature often includes wonder, excitement, joy, awe, and feelings of inner peace. Children soon discover deep connections with other living things and an awareness of the interconnectedness found within the natural world. Such discoveries instill a sense of wonder and awe and lead to amazing questions, deeper learning, and eventually provide children with a growing ability to feel empathy, caring, and kindness toward others.

The following suggestions for promoting children's spiritual development while they are engaged in nature are based on Schein's approach to working with young children. She suggests that parents and educators should:

- ✿ value the time children spend outdoors as spiritual moments. This means that children need time to just be in nature, with no agenda, with no directions given. Let the child be her own guide.

- ✿ invite children to watch a thunderstorm from a window or go for a walk in the rain. After it rains, wonder together with children, "Where does the wetness go? What happened to the puddle of water?" If you are lucky, you might catch a bird taking a bath in a puddle after a rain.

- ✿ help children notice relationships among sun, shade, and shadows. Make body shapes with sun and shadows.

- ✿ take a picture of an awesome natural place or happening and talk about it with a child. Have children choose a nature picture that they like, and repeat the process.

- ✿ have children observe their own breathing, the breathing of someone else, and the breathing of an animal or a baby.

- ✿ watch the wind move the leaves in the trees and laugh as it carries a kite far above your heads.

- ✿ sit quietly with your child as you observe a sunrise or a sunset.

✿ encourage an ecological perspective. For example, view a situation from the point of view of a plant, an animal, a river, a mountain, and other elements of the natural world. You might say, "The baby bird must be so excited to see its mother coming back with food."

✿ expose children to the beauty of nature in many different forms, such as in art, music, and poetry, especially while enjoying an outdoor space.

✿ add plants, river rocks, leaves, and other natural materials to the indoor environment and invite children to touch, move, and play with these items.

✿ provide picture books with beautiful illustrations of nature.

✿ demonstrate gratitude and appreciation for the many gifts of nature: strawberries, shiny pebbles, crumbly leaves.

✿ engage children in the care of plants, animals, and ecosystems.

✿ give children the opportunity to witness the wonders of nature through experiences such as planting a seed and watching it grow or observing the process of a tadpole transforming into a frog.

✿ call attention to the spiritual aspects of beauty and place: "Let's sit under the tree for a while. It's such a peaceful place."

✿ invite children to find their own special places and then share them with others, but only when the children are ready to do so!

✿ model and encourage a serene mind while observing the sounds, sights, and happenings of the natural world. Serenity can become a precursor to curiosity, inquiry, and excitement for learning and deepening one's relationship with nature. Serenity can lead to kindness and empathy.

✿ engage children in meaningful dialogue about the wonders and mysteries of nature. Spending time in meaningful dialogue about nature can lead to big questions and help a child feel part of something larger than herself.

✿ encourage children to draw, paint, sculpt, and write about their impressions of and experiences with nature, adapting these activities for children with special needs. Use art to enhance the integrated power of nature, spirituality, beauty, expression, and creativity. It is up to parents and educators to provide ways for all children to engage!

- For a child with a visual impairment, provide bright markers or paint to contrast with paper. Provide real natural materials, such as leaves, stones, seed pods, and flowers, rather than pictures of such materials.

- For a child with a hearing impairment, pair oral directions with a visual model of the process.

- For a child with physical impairments, provide adaptive art tools, such as chunky crayons and large markers.

- For a child with attention-deficit and/or behavioral concerns, offer materials such as clay or playdough to use to express feelings, insights, and energy, and give them plenty of time to be outdoors where attention and behavioral issues are less of a concern and sometimes less noticeable to the child and to others.

- Most importantly, have fun, play, and share with others while outdoors!

The term *holistic* is sometimes used in reference to human activities focusing on the integration of body, mind, and spirit. We find this descriptor applied to different facets of our lives, such as holistic health, holistic architecture, holistic pregnancy and childbirth, holistic vacations, and holistic education. As used in these contexts, *holistic* generally includes the concept of connections between the physical and nonphysical. These connections may be between scientific and intuitive ways of knowing, between individual and community and between humans and the rest of the natural world. Whether clearly stated or not, as used in these different contexts, *holistic* includes a nonphysical or spiritual component.

REFLECTIONS: THE WORLD AS A "VALE OF SOUL-MAKING"

The terms *spirit* and *soul* are sometimes used interchangeably in reference to an integral dimension of who we are as humans. This dimension—which may or may not be nurtured through religion—can be fostered through rich nature-related experiences. We might call these "soul-making" experiences.

While some thinkers and writers have referred to this world as a "vale of tears"—a place where we must struggle, work, and suffer—the poet John Keats suggested that we live in a "Vale of Soul-Making"—that is, a place that breathes life and a sense of wonder into our beings. Young children seem to be especially in tune with the spiritual dimensions of nature. They seldom experience nature simply as a stage or backdrop for their activities. Children interact *with* the world of nature; they don't just act *on* it. They're connected to nature, not just physically but also emotionally and spiritually. Children's interactions with nature are often filled with joy, wonder, and awe. We see that nature touches their spirits in deep and profound ways. Rat in *The Wind in the Willows* by Kenneth Grahame expresses it well: "This is the place of my song-dream, the place the music played to me." The place Rat refers to is "the flowery margin of the island . . . a marvelous green, set round with Nature's own orchard trees."

I am reminded of some of my own childhood experiences. I remember experiencing the world as a marvelous place for adventure and exploration, for discovering beauty and mystery. I grew up on an eighty-acre farm, immersed in the world of nature. I fed the chickens and watered the garden. I picked cherries and plums from the trees in our yard. I watched the corn grow tall and the tomatoes ripen in the field. I played in the woods and marveled at the way wildflowers emerged from the ground each spring. I remember such experiences as being magical; they filled my world with song. The memory of these experiences continues to enrich my life today.

~~~~~~~~~~~~~~~~

PROGRAM SPOTLIGHT
SOL FOREST SCHOOL*

As I head up the rocky, mountainous trail to visit a group of young children learning under the Ponderosa canopy, excitement and joy ring through the air. This is SOL Forest School, based in the East Mountains outside Albuquerque, New Mexico. SOL is a preschool, and classes are held entirely outdoors in a forest setting. The curriculum is based on children's interests and what the forest has to offer. Adults—including a teacher certified in forest school pedagogy—serve as collaborators in the children's play and learning. SOL has only one "rule" and that is to care. Teachers, families, and the children themselves can be heard negotiating social situations or rough play that may harm a plant or other living being by using this rule. They show care towards themselves, their friends, their belongings, their forest classroom, and the other-than-human world living there.

SOL is a proud member of the American Forest Kindergarten Association and follows the forest school pedagogy, which is child directed, play based, held entirely outdoors year-round, and always in rhythm with the seasons and the multiple emergent interests that unfold when one works with nature as coteacher. SOL is also "soul-based"; SOL stands for "soulful outdoor learning."

Sally Anderson, the founder and director of SOL Forest School, explains how high-energy activities are balanced with mindful moments. The intent is to promote all aspects of the child, including the spiritual, or soulful, aspects. Sally and her coteachers encourage children to not only climb the trees but to develop a special relationship with them. Sally refers to the children as *treeschoolers* and to the trees as friends. She encourages children to listen to the trees, to each other, and to themselves. She gives them time to take in the beauty, peace, and intricacy of the natural world. When the treeschoolers bring subjects they are trying to understand in their daily lives, such as significant talk around Black Lives Matter and the rights of Black people or Indigenous People of Color, Sally will ask, "How do you think the trees see us? Do you think they view one group of people as being better or different than another?"

As a certified shinrin-yoku forest therapy guide, Sally is well aware of the benefits of taking in the forest through the senses. She sees herself as "opening the door, but the forest provides the medicine." Spending time in the trees reduces stress, promotes healthy immune-system functioning, instills a sense of calm, and rejuvenates the spirit. Sally sees the positive effect the forest has on the children as they interact with the forest environment and with each other. She sees how easy it is for them to joyfully be in their bodies as feeling, sensing humans, and she loves guiding adults through her shinrin-yoku practice in "remembering" this embodied sense of joy. Sally and her staff witness frequent expressions of wonder and wondering, of observing and caring. As children engage deeply with nature—physically, mentally, and emotionally—they come to a kind of knowing that tells them they are part of the forest, a part of the entire world of nature. This is "soulful knowing" that emerges through the SOL Forest School experience.

*Based on observations during a personal visit to SOL and an interview with Sally Anderson in 2020

Living life holistically includes the experience of being immersed in the beauty and wonder of nature. It includes the experience of everyday spirituality—a spirituality rooted in wisdom and compassion, wonder and joy, connections and belonging.

This chapter discussed ways in which nature promotes the holistic development of children, with special sections devoted to ecological identity and spiritual health, as these areas of holistic development are often overlooked in the early childhood literature. The next chapter focuses on natural environments and ways in which the resources they have to offer encourage children of differing abilities to play, explore, and learn.

REFERENCES

Bakir-Demir, Tugce, Sibel Kazak Berument, and Basak Sahin-Acar. 2019. "The Relationship Between Greenery and Self-Regulation of Children: The Mediation Role of Nature Connectedness." *Journal of Environmental Psychology* 65: 101327.

Baxter, Daniel, and Luc Pelletier. 2018. "Is Nature Relatedness a Basic Human Psychological Need? A Critical Examination of the Extant Literature." *Canadian Psychology* 60(1): 21–34.

Cheng, Judith, and Martha Monroe. 2012. "Connection to Nature: Children's Affective Attitude Toward Nature." *Environment and Behavior* 44(1): 31–49.

Cleary, Anne, et al. 2017. "Exploring Potential Mechanisms Involved in the Relationship between Eudaimonic Wellbeing and Nature Connection." *Landscape and Urban Planning* 158: 119–128.

Dennis, Samuel, Christine Kiewra, and Alexandra Wells. 2019. *Natural Outdoor Classrooms: A National Survey Final Report. Dimensions Foundation.* https://dimensionsfoundation.org/research/research-findings/

Grahame, Kenneth. 1908. *The Wind in the Willows.* Slingsby, York, England, UK: Methuen Publishing, Ltd.

Green, Carie. 2016. "Sensory Tours as a Method for Engaging Children as Active Researchers:

Exploring the Use of Wearable Cameras in Early Childhood Research." *International Journal of Early Childhood* 48(3): 277–294.

Green, Carie, Darius Kalvaitis, and Anneliese Worster. 2016. "Recontextualizing Psychosocial Development in Young Children: A Model of Environmental Identity Development." *Environmental Education Research* 22(7): 1025–1048.

Green, Carie. 2017. "Children's Environmental Identity Development in an Alaska Native Rural

Context." *International Journal of Early Childhood* 49(3): 303–319.

Green, Carie. 2018. *Children's Environmental Identity Development: Negotiating Inner and Outer Tensions in Natural World Socialization.* New York: Peter Lang.

Hawks, Steven. 1994. "Spiritual Health: Definition and Theory." *Wellness Perspectives* 10(4): 3–13.

Heintzman, Paul. 2014. "Nature-Based Recreation, Spirituality, and Persons with Disabilities." *Journal of Disability and Religion* 18(1): 97–116.

Lumber, Ryan, Miles Richardson, and David Sheffield, D. 2018. "The Seven Pathways to Nature Connectedness: A Focus Group Exploration." *European Journal of Ecopsychology* 6: 47–48.

Nisbet, Elizabeth K., John Zelenski, and Steven Murphy. 2009. "The Nature Relatedness Scale: Linking Individuals' Connection with Nature to Environmental Concern and Behavior." *Environment and Behavior* 41(5): 715–740.

Pritchard, Alison, et al. 2019. "The Relationship Between Nature Connectedness and Eudaimonic Well-Being: A Meta-Analysis." *Journal of Happiness Studies* 21(3):1145–1167.

Rosenow, Nancy. 2012. *Heart-Centered Teaching Inspired by Nature: Using Nature's Wisdom to Bring More Joy and Effectiveness to Our Work with Children*. Lincoln, NE: Dimensions Educational Research Foundation

Sobko, Tanja, Zhenzhen Jia, and Gavin Brown. 2018. "Measuring Connectedness to Nature in Preschool Children in an Urban Setting and Its Relation to Psychological Functioning." *PLoS ONE* 13(11): e0207057.

Wilson, Ruth. 2011. "The Making of Beautiful People." *Exchange* 33(6): 45–49.

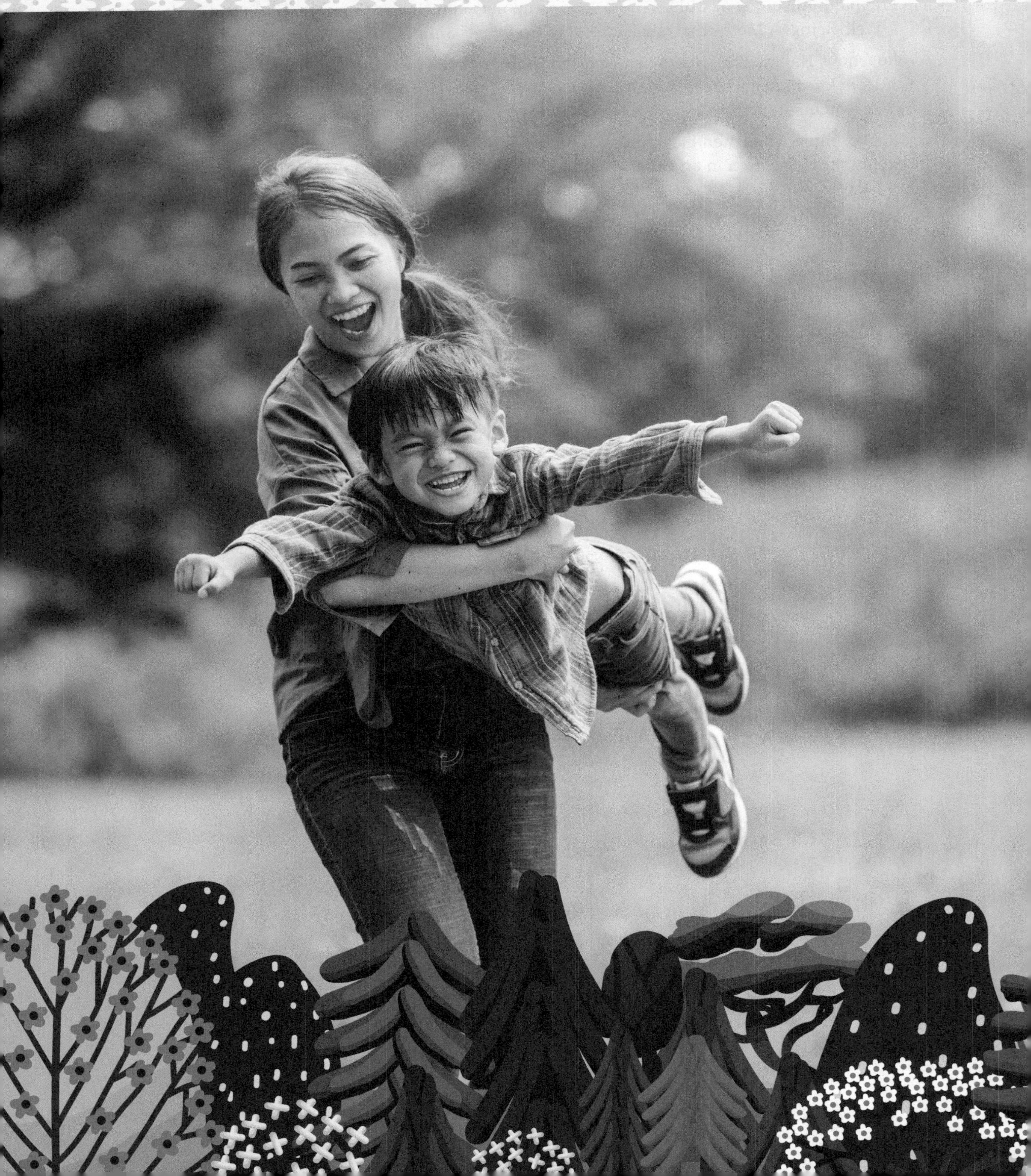

CHAPTER 8

Connecting Through Natural Environments

"

Nature is our natural habitat.

— **RUTH WILSON**,
The Commons—A Place for Kids

The Rio Grande *bosque* (Spanish for "forest") is one of the most beautiful and most loved open-space areas in Albuquerque, New Mexico. Here, the river and large cottonwood trees, coyote willow, and New Mexico olive provide habitat for beaver, turtles, snakes, porcupines, and numerous species of birds. A shady sixteen-mile multi-use path running through the bosque is popular with hikers, bikers, skaters, bird watchers, photographers, and nature lovers of all ages.

Yet, a complaint registered with the city alleges that there are too many children laughing and enjoying the bosque during summer vacation. Debate over who should have access to open space and how it should be used is not new. So, whom do the bosque and other open-space areas really belong to? Are children included?

A look at a typical city suggests that children should enjoy their time outdoors in places designed specifically for them. We call such places *playgrounds* and often enclose them with fences. This arrangement conveys the idea that children should be confined to certain places while enjoying the outdoors. Yet, this arrangement isn't what children really want and need. The design of many playgrounds is sadly deficient in meeting the physical, social, and emotional needs of children.

What children want and need are opportunities to explore, discover, and make a place their own. Playgrounds—where equipment is usually anchored in cement and designed to be used in a certain way—fail to invite much exploration and creativity. In terms of playability, empty lots with an abundance of mud, moss, weeds, and bugs have more to offer than traditional playgrounds. Unfortunately, children's access to empty lots and other natural areas is becoming ever more restricted. The result—as Jay Griffiths says in *Kith: The Riddle of the Childscape*—is that childhood is losing its commons.

Kith is from an Old English word meaning "native land." It also means kinsfolk, neighbors, or people who live near you but aren't blood relatives. For purposes of this discussion, however, *kith* is used in reference to public open space—or the *commons*—which, in earlier times, served as a play space and a sort of "home away from home" for many children. Griffiths suggests that the loss of the kith is one of the main contributors to children's unhappiness. She discusses how children today are generally impoverished by being exiled from nature, which was once abundantly available to them in the kith.

Factors contributing to this loss include the actual disappearance of open space and attitudes about what children should and should not be doing. Suggesting that children should be at home watching TV or playing video games rather than enjoying the bosque is one example of an attitude inconsistent with what is in the best interests of children. Families who are overanxious about the safety of their children and children who are overprogrammed in their daily lives also contribute to children's diminishing access to interactions with nature. A childhood spent indoors generally leads to adults knowing little about the larger place they inhabit. A childhood spent indoors is also more likely to be a childhood with diminished happiness.

This chapter discusses the importance of providing child-friendly outdoor spaces where children can play, explore, and learn. It also provides some suggestions for developing natural play spaces for young children and discusses ways in which natural environments promote active explorations and rich socially interactive play.

Increasing Children's Access to Nature

Fortunately, initiatives are underway in many places around the world to make the commons more inviting and accessible to children. One such initiative focuses on providing natural playspaces for children. A *natural playspace* is a space intentionally designed to include natural features for play and active exploration. Natural features, such as rocks, logs, sand, and soil, are already present in many open-space areas. The problem is that, in many places, the rule is "Do not disturb," a rule that includes restrictions about moving things about in the physical environment. In the case of the complaint about children in the bosque, this also includes not disturbing the peace and quiet some other users (adults) are seeking. Thus, the conflict of interests.

The Natural Learning Initiative (NLI) at North Carolina State University is a nationally and internationally recognized leader in making natural playspaces available to children. NLI works with community institutions and organizations, including schools, child-care centers, parks, museums, and neighborhoods, to create stimulating outdoor places for play and learning.

The nature-play movement is another initiative making the commons more inviting to children. Children engaged in nature play dig in the dirt, pour water over sand and stones, use branches and sticks to build forts, make mud soup, and float leaves in a stream. NatureStart, a professional-development program of the Chicago Zoological Society, is a leader in the nature-play movement. NatureStart works with zoos, aquariums, nature centers, and other informal learning institutions around the globe to provide nature-play opportunities for young children. At times, this involves changing the rules about how open space can be used. The development of the Nature Play Zone at the Indiana Dunes National Park is one example of an established organization developing new policies to make open space more accessible to children.

One of the park rangers at Indiana Dunes National Park participated in a NatureStart program at Brookfield Zoo. Excited about the possibilities, she envisioned a nature-play area at the park where she worked. To make this happen, however, policy and procedural changes were necessary, as a general rule for national parks is "Do not disturb." Fortunately, the needed policy changes were made, and in April 2013, the Nature Play Zone welcomed its first visitors. Today, children and their caregivers can build sand forts, climb trees, scoop water and sand in buckets, and engage in all types of imaginative play with natural materials while visiting the park.

Cities Connecting Children to Nature (CCCN) is also working to engage children with nature experiences. This initiative represents a partnership between the National League of Cities, the Children & Nature Network, other nonprofit organizations, and the private sector. A part of this initiative involves greening schoolyards and the outdoor play spaces of child-care centers. The process generally involves adding different types of vegetation, sand and soil, and possibly water to a playground. This initiative also includes working with city planners and other community groups to incorporate nature play and learning spaces into the green infrastructure of the city, thereby addressing the play deserts that exist in too many cities. The term *play desert* refers to neighborhoods lacking child-friendly spaces for physical activity and active play. A child who must travel miles to get to the nearest park or child-friendly open space lives in a play desert.

Playability is a concept with important implications for children's enjoyment of the commons. Play is what children do. To enjoy the commons, they need places with play potential. Unfortunately, not all children have access to such places. When considering play settings for children, keep in mind that children need places, not just spaces. Traditional playgrounds are designed by adults and tend to favor order and efficiency; they are spaces. Children, on the other hand, are more likely to be comfortable with informality and unstructured activity, preferring places with ample opportunities for exploration.

Many child-care centers and schools do not have a forest or other natural environment in their backyard and may have only limited space and funds for naturalizing their outdoor environment. While there are many creative and inexpensive ways to add natural materials to the indoor and outdoor places where young children play and learn, partnering with environmental organizations is another way to expand children's opportunities for nature-rich experiences. Patti Ensel Bailie, former director of the Schlitz Audubon Nature Preschool and current associate professor of early childhood education at the University of Maine at Farmington, offers suggestions on how early childhood teachers and environmental educators can work together to help young children make positive connections to the natural world. Her suggestions revolve around the idea of a continuum, ranging from a one-hour field trip at one end to a licensed, nature-based preschool at the other end. Examples of other types of programs falling between these two ends of the continuum include seasonal field trips, teacher workshops, and family programs.

Miriam Murphy, Youth and Family Programs Inclusion Coordinator at the Morton Arboretum in Lisle, Illinois, hosted a field trip of a group of children who were deafblind. Her story (on page 117) illustrates how a field trip helps children make positive connections with the natural world.

☀

Natural Playspaces

The term *natural environment* is often used in reference to a place that has been minimally affected by human activity. A natural environment stands in contrast to a built environment that humans have shaped. Distinctions between the natural environment and the built environment are somewhat arbitrary. For example, we might consider a wetland a natural environment, yet a close examination will reveal signs of human impact, even if the wetland is located in a remote area. Similarly, we might consider our homes a built environment, yet we often find elements of the natural world there—a spider in a closet, a tree in the yard, or a toad underneath a back-porch light.

PROGRAM SPOTLIGHT
MORTON ARBORETUM CHILDREN'S GARDEN

One brisk autumn morning, two buses arrived near the visitor center. Some of the students rode in wheelchairs, while some walked with assistance from teachers or therapists on the paved path leading to the children's garden. We were bundled for the weather but grinning as we all filled our lungs with the fresh morning air. Our team had partnered with a local school to facilitate a visit to the children's garden for a group of students who are members of the DeafBlind community. Our visitors had varying levels of hearing and sight, so we reflected on ways to make it a meaningful experience for all. Inspired by tactile signing, a mode of communication used by some in the DeafBlind community, I wondered how we could engage our sense of touch as one way to explore the garden.

Near the entrance, the garden beds were filled with lamb's ear, which enthralled both the students and the accompanying staff with its soft leaves, perhaps providing a nostalgic similarity to a cherished stuffed animal or a beloved blanket. As we made our way up the curved path to Adventure Woods, we were greeted by Wonder Pond. Some students crouched down on the boardwalks to get closer to the water. They felt the initial tension as their palms met the surface of the pond followed by a cool flow of water running between their fingers. Then, following the paths, the students began to differentiate between the smooth asphalt and the crunch of the fallen leaves beneath their feet.

After our joyous parade back down the path, we met under the picnic shelter to continue our exploration. Each table held a sensory bin filled with tree seeds, tree cookies, and leaves from white oaks, maples, and hickories. Some of the leaves were laminated to reinforce the stems, veins, and tips, which provided an opportunity for the students to experiment with leaf rubbings. Each student was also given a tactile scavenger-hunt book that included various materials, such as felt, sandpaper, twine, fabric, and bark, to simulate textures found in nature. Each texture was glued to a piece of card stock and attached to a paper bag; then these were bound together to form a book. This way, if the student found a similar texture while exploring, he or she could keep this natural treasure in a bag.

As one student brushed his hand across the piece of bark, he was suddenly reminded of the strong, rough armor surrounding the trunks of trees. He was determined to find a tree he could embrace. Our sense of touch connects us to nature, but it is being touched by nature that connects us to one another.

There are obviously varying degrees of naturalness in the environments in which children live, play, and learn. Consider the difference between children's experience of nature in a forest and what they would experience on an asphalt-covered playground with swings and slides. Children rarely, if ever, spend time in an environment that's entirely natural. Yet, biodiverse environments, even though they're not entirely natural, can provide many opportunities for rich nature engagement.

As discussed in previous chapters, nature engagement is a strong contributor to children's development and learning and may be especially important for children with special needs. Research shows that the benefits to young children with special needs of playing and exploring in natural environments includes more peer interaction as well as peer teaching (Cloward Drown and Christensen, 2014).

Sylvia Collazo, an early childhood educator, observed how Karma blossomed when she was in a nature playspace.

> Years ago, I had the opportunity to work with an amazing family and their beautiful daughter, Karma. When we first met, she kept mostly to herself, often clinging to her mother during the Baby Signs sessions I hosted in my home. Her bright eyes, always observant, watched me, the moms, and their little ones engage in our weekly stories, games, and songs. Sometimes, she ventured past her mother's lap and came toward me to play; those were some of the best moments in class. Although she didn't say much, her mother joyfully shared that Karma was beginning to use signs at home.
>
> When it was time to meet for our last class, themed "At the Park," it was clear we had to be outside. Unfortunately (or perhaps fortunately), Karma and her mother were the only ones who made it out to the class that day. As soon as I spotted them standing just outside the playground, the magic of nature began! My once-shy little friend ran over to me and hugged my neck like a long-lost companion. She was beaming. It was as if being outside had granted her the permission to freely be and express herself.
>
> We walked over to her mom, who stood astonished at her little girl's actions. Karma had never done that before with anyone except family. Excitedly, we started our class in the playground area where I watched Karma check out the swings and enjoy her first time on a slide. We then explored the park, where I shared signs for the tall palm trees, the people walking dogs, and the butterflies perching on wildflowers. Karma's grin widened with everything she saw, and when she spotted ducks swimming in the nearby pond, she even started using signs she remembered from before. Originally scheduled as a 45-minute class, the three of us spent well over an hour walking, talking, signing, and enjoying all that nature had to offer that day.
>
> From my personal experiences with nature, I knew it was a place where I often found refuge from the noise and felt most at peace. Over my years of teaching young children with developmental delays, I had introduced nature to my students by visiting local parks and the city zoo, digging in dirt and growing plants, and taking nature walks around the school's fence line. That day at the park with Karma, however, I had the opportunity to step back and observe so many examples of how nature could support young children's development.

Although I knew her mother worried about possible language and social delays, I watched Karma blossom during her time outdoors. In attending to, engaging, and communicating with her environment and those around her, she demonstrated some of the key benefits of spending time in nature that have been uncovered by research, even among children with different needs.

Natural playspaces can provide comfort and relaxation for children with special needs and their caregivers. Such environments also provide sensory stimulation that supports children's multiple learning abilities, sustains their interests, and encourages cooperative activities that can promote positive social behaviors. In the following vignette, Rachel Tenney, an early childhood special-education teacher in New York City, reflects on how natural playspaces benefit young children with special needs:

Time outdoors provides a welcome alternative to the more limiting behavioral expectations of an indoor environment. Features of the outdoor natural environment place "reasonable limitations" on a child's behavior. These limitations are less socially constructed and more easily understood by the child. The child can sense safety-related limitations and test their own capabilities. The outdoor environment also provides opportunities for success as this relates to expectations. Indoors, the child is usually expected to attend to the social environment. This includes listening to what the teacher is saying and attending to a task at hand. Outdoors, the child is free to attend to environmental sounds and situations. Listening to a bird in a tree, for example, is something the child can enjoy. The child can experience success in identifying the source of the sound.

The outdoor environment also allows for successful negotiations with peers. Indoors, the materials for joint activities tend to be limited in number and prescribed in terms of use. Natural materials outdoors are unending and their use unprescribed. This allows for successful interaction in joint activities. And the diverse features and materials of a natural outdoor environment allow for a wide variety of activities. Some children may enjoy playing with mud; others may find touching mud repugnant. A child who is averse to mud may enjoy pulling seed pods apart or picking strawberries as they ripen.

Children who find adjusting to change difficult may benefit from observing the changes in nature. Elements of the natural world are always changing but tend to do so in a somewhat predictable manner. As children return to the same place over time, they can notice what remains and what changes. Such observations can help children prepare for changes in their lives.

The power of nature to affect children in positive ways may reflect an innate affinity—or kinship—children have with the other-than-human parts of nature. This affinity, however, may need to be nurtured. Children with behavioral challenges may need more adult guidance than some other children while relating to nature. For example, a child who tends to throw and hit things when stressed may need to observe bugs in a bug jar rather than on his or her hand. Young children may also need adult support in learning to treat critters with respect. Adult modeling can extend a child's circle of concern. This occurred with one child who was afraid of dragonflies. The day after participating in the burial of a dead dragonfly, this child wanted to visit the grave to see if the dragonfly had a good sleep.

Naturalizing a Playspace

Early childhood educators might have to work with a not-so-natural playspace; however, that isn't too hard to fix. Consider the following ideas and resources to naturalize your playspace.

✿ **Basic features:**

- **Plentiful and varied vegetation:** Native trees, bushes, flowers, and so forth attract and provide habitat for native wildlife. Some of the vegetation should have low, leafy foliage for the children to touch. Some should change with the seasons. Avoid plants that may be poisonous.

- **Varied ground cover, including sand and soil:** Sand and soil are basic elements that children can manipulate. Consider adding water to these elements to increase the play and learning potential.

- **Animals:** Both domesticated and wild animals make an environment more interesting to children. Animals can also promote empathy, ecological perspective, connectedness to nature, kinship, and a sense of wonder. Provide bird feeders, birdbaths, nesting boxes, organic residue on the ground such as decaying leaves, and other sources of food and shelter to encourage wildlife to your playspace. Use fencing and sheds to house domestic animals, such as chickens and goats.

- **A variety of levels and nooks:** Slopes, mounds, and terraces give children the opportunity to view an area from different levels, promote learning, and add interest to play. Nooks in different places throughout a playspace offer varied opportunities for socialization, privacy, relaxation, rest, and views.

- **Diversity in ground surfaces and ground-level components:** Diversity in what children experience and can access at ground level, such as the scents of flowers and other plants, the feel of rocks and soil, the taste of berries, the coolness of shade, and the wetness of dew and bodies of water, can engage their imaginations and curiosity and offer a variety of play activities.

- **Shady areas:** Children will need some shade for comfort and health. Experiencing differences between shady and sunny areas can also be instructive.

- **Loose parts:** Open-ended natural materials, such as plant parts, sand, and stones, along with tools, such as shovels and buckets, and props, such as kitchen utensils, stimulate curiosity and imagination. Loose materials encourage children to engage in all types of play.

- **Accessible routes and access points to different parts of the playspace:** A circular pathway design can provide access to all activity areas. During the design process, consider ramps, accessible ground cover, and space for maneuvering.

- **Settings and materials that invite peer interaction:** Wagons and a swing or bench built for several children can invite peer interaction.

- **Settings and materials that provide appropriate challenge and risk:** Risky play, which offers children the thrill of uncertainty, encourages physical activity, social interaction, and exploration and understanding of the world. It's important to note that *risk* and *hazard* are not the same. *Risk,* in the context of play, refers to environmental challenges and uncertainties that a child can recognize and learn to manage based on a determination of his or her own limits (Brussoni et al., 2017). *Hazard,* in the context of play, refers to something that is dangerous and likely to cause harm.

✿ **Optional Features:**

- **Barefoot area/barefoot course:** Walking barefoot in nature helps children develop the sense of touch in the feet, strengthens the arches, and promotes normal gait patterns and balance (Hanscom, 2016). Grass, soft moss, clay, sand, smooth stones, and mud can all serve as barefoot walking materials.

- **Slopes and dips:** Topography with slopes and dips allows children to practice their balance and explore their center of gravity.

- **Garden area:** If your play area includes a garden, encourage children to be actively engaged in the garden activities: preparing the soil, harvesting the produce, and consuming fruits and vegetables grown on-site.

- **Musical instruments:** Musical instruments in outdoor playspaces tend to be used frequently by children. As some children may be sensitive to loud noises, disperse musical equipment throughout the playground to reduce the level of sound in one location. Consider choosing musical instruments that produce low tones, because some children with auditory oversensitivity may be uncomfortable with high-pitched sounds.

- **Art studio:** An area set up as an art studio could include easels, clipboards, paper, chalk, paints, and clay.

- **Performance stage:** A stage area encourages a variety of dramatic play, with opportunities for children with varying abilities to be actively engaged.

- **Wildlife area:** A wildlife area might take the form of a butterfly garden, a mini-beast habitat or bug hotel, a bird-feeding station, or a small pond.

- **Moveable manufactured objects:** Wagons, buckets, blocks, wheelbarrows, and riding toys invite physical activity and different types of play. Such objects tend to draw children into more active engagement with the natural environment.

- **Tables or workbenches:** While children can use tree stumps as writing or drawing surfaces, it's also helpful to have tables or workbenches in a playspace.

- **Playhouse or play cabin:** Tents, vine teepees, and sunflower forts can be used instead of, or in addition to, a playhouse. Such enclosures invite social and dramatic play.

- **Mud kitchen:** Use a variety of materials to set up a mud kitchen, with a giant spool or a pile of bricks to serve as its base.

- **Rock pile:** A pile of rocks of various sizes invites constructive, dramatic, and social play. Children can use the rocks for stacking, carrying, making "roads," defining a space, and so on.
- **Compost bin:** Use wire enclosures, large buckets, and other types of containers for compost, and include children in the composting process.

Universal Design in Natural Environments

Kathryn Hunt Baker, a nature-based educator and consultant kindergarten teacher at Turn Back Time farm and nature-based program in Paxton, Massachusetts, offers the following reflection on the value of using Universal Design:

> Universal Design is based on the idea that accommodating features are beneficial to more than those who require an accommodation, and that it is efficient to consider accommodations when designing and developing new programs and spaces. In construction, this translates to considering compliance with the Americans with Disabilities Act (ADA) in the design phase to avoid costs of retrofitting if the needs for accommodations arise.
>
> A building designed according to ADA guidelines might include a sloped ramp at the entry rather than stairs. This is an obvious accommodation for patrons who use wheelchairs but is one that is also useful for families with strollers, delivery persons, the elderly, and people who are fatigued. It is expensive to replace stairs with ramps if the need arises, so a building constructed using Universal Design theory can save money in addition to making the building more welcoming to people with varying needs and abilities.
>
> In education, Universal Design for Learning (UDL) provides resources and adaptations for not only the children who require an accommodation but for all children, with the idea that the accommodation might benefit more broadly. For example, a classroom that uses UDL might include games, strategies, and technology that deliver content to support learners with learning differences, rather than extracting the children with special needs to a separate environment. By making alternative learning strategies flexible and available to all children, you not only support the child who has a defined need but introduce strategies that support children who don't have a defined diagnosis but would benefit from alternative strategies.
>
> With an understanding of accommodations and needs, we can translate Universal Design theory into nature-based education as well. Turn Back Time, a nature-based education program in Massachusetts, is where this happens regularly—in the physical learning environment, program development, and curriculum development. By looking at how the program utilizes this theory in its program, early childhood educators can learn how they might be able to do so in their programs as well.

- **Physical learning environment:** When creating paths or hiking trails, staff members at Turn Back Time make sure these are at least 36 inches wide. Create clear pathways between defined spaces whenever possible, and seek the flattest terrain when creating new trails or provide alternative walkways for challenging ones. Play areas are located where there is a combination of flat ground and varying terrain. By creating and accessing spaces in this way, staff ensure that they can be more inclusive for people with physical differences and avoid the need to retrofit spaces for individual children as they enroll.

  Occasionally, you will find some places that just don't work for all children of all needs. For instance, at Turn Back Time we have a destination called Forest Town that the children developed much in the way of the beloved children's book *Roxaboxen* by Alice McLerran. Forest Town offers community play, an opportunity to build shelters, and a sense of ownership; however, the terrain to get there is challenging. The hike is a fair distance up a steep slope, over a creek, and through dense brush. The staff at Turn Back Time realized that accommodating this terrain for children who have motor challenges was more than we could undertake. Instead, teachers spent time observing what Forest Town offers children and made sure to offer similar experiences. We ended up developing Kindergarten Town and Enrichment Playground—smaller spaces closer to the home bases that meet the needs for children who might have mobility challenges or other individual needs while still offering the rich community play and feeling of ownership observed in Forest Town.

- **Program development:** The staff at Turn Back Time considers possible accommodations when planning its "flow," or structure, of the day, so that we can provide all children with the least-restrictive environment, taking skill, ability, and energy levels into account. The program staff consider materials suited for a wide range of abilities and make all ranges of materials accessible for all children. We place extra staff in class groups or areas to make sure that every child's needs are met. We meet regularly to reflect upon classroom dynamics, the needs of children, and staff support. Considering these details in the planning stages of program development creates a level of flexibility and opportunity for any child who might enroll in the program.

- **Curriculum development:** Turn Back Time's emergent-curriculum model allows for support of all learners, as emergent teaching supports Universal Design for Learning. The nature of an emergent curriculum is that it is designed around the individual needs, abilities, and interests of the children. Emergent curriculum is a pedagogy where teachers look for the interests of the children to develop a curriculum tailored specifically to them. This way of teaching is exciting and creates strong connections between the learner and the content. With an emergent curriculum, accommodations for specific children are naturally part of the process and are available to all the children in the program.

Physical Health and Development Benefits of Natural Environments

Previous chapters addressed some of the cognitive, social, emotional, and spiritual benefits of natural environments for children. This section focuses more specifically on the physical health and development benefits children gain by playing and exploring in natural environments. These benefits include the promotion of gross- and fine-motor skills, sensory integration, and improved immune functioning. Playing and exploring in natural environments also engages a child's proprioceptive and vestibular senses, helping them with motor functioning.

Children need to develop both gross-motor and fine-motor skills to do many of the things children do: run, walk, climb, hold a pencil, brush teeth, and pick flowers. As Angela Hanscom (2016) indicates, these skills are honed when the muscles, brain, and nervous system work together to allow a child to perform a physical action. This honing requires daily practice.

GROSS- AND FINE-MOTOR SKILLS

Children need to practice using their large muscles to develop both precision and strength. Precision involves control and coordination of their physical movements. Strength involves endurance and contributes to postural control. Activities in natural environments that promote gross-motor skills include climbing trees, walking through mud puddles, stepping over logs, raking leaves, digging in the garden, and picking apples.

Once children attain a certain amount of muscle strength and body stability, they get better at manipulating objects in their environment. Their small muscle movements become more precise, and they move from just swatting at an object to grasping it. Accomplishing more complex tasks, such as holding a spoon to put food in one's mouth, requires the ability to do more than grasp an object. It takes coordination. Children develop coordination by using fingers and hands in a variety of ways. Activities in natural environments that promote fine-motor skills include planting seeds, picking flowers, making fairy houses, and sculpting with mud or wet sand.

SENSORY PROCESSING

In this section, occupational therapist Jennifer Rosinia, PhD, OTR/L, shares information about how young children learn through their senses and how sensory processing helps them organize and use sensory information. She also shares a story about Jameson and his sensory processing disorder.

> Young children learn through their senses. Actually, the role of sensory input is primary throughout all of human development. The theory of sensory integration, which includes specific sensory-based treatment strategies, was created, researched, and developed by occupational therapist Dr. A. Jean Ayres. *Sensory integration* is the neurological process that organizes

sensations from one's own body and the environment and makes it possible to use the body effectively within the environment. When learning about the sensory systems, the basic five senses of sight, smell, taste, hearing, and touch are typically taught; however, there are really eight sensory systems. Two of these lesser-known sensory systems are related to movement: the proprioceptive system and the vestibular system.

The *proprioceptive system* receives information from the body's muscles, joints, and ligaments. This sense lets a child know where his body parts are and what they are doing. Information provided by this system tells a child how far to reach to pick a flower, how high to lift a foot to step on a log, and how much force to use to pick up and carry a heavy log. When children are engaged in proprioceptive activities, those activities are frequently referred to as *heavy work*.

The *vestibular system* plays a role in a child's balance by providing information as to the position of the head and body in relation to the earth and objects in the environment. This system supports a person's coordination, the ability to move both sides of the body together, coordinated eye movements, as well as arousal, attention, and emotional states. Balancing on stepping stones while crossing a creek or hanging upside down and swinging from a branch are made possible by the vestibular system.

These two systems are intimately connected, so much so that when a child manipulates natural loose materials, such as gathering and using stones to build a tower or stirring leaves in a heavy bucket of water to make "tea" or "soup," both the vestibular and proprioceptive sensory systems are engaged. Natural environments promote the development of the proprioceptive and vestibular senses in young children and serve to regulate their nervous systems.

Recently, the term *sensory processing* has been used interchangeably with term *sensory integration*. While each of these terms refer to the body's reception, organization, and use of sensory information, they are subtly different in important ways.

Sensory integration refers to a specific theory that informs the therapeutic practices of occupational therapists. *Sensory processing*, on the other hand, is a more generalized term that is used by a variety of professionals. Sensory processing refers to the way the nervous system receives sensory messages and turns them into responses. Some individuals, such as Olympic athletes, are great at sensory processing. Most of us are good enough at processing our sensory world and do not experience disturbances that negatively affect our relationships or learning. Then there are those for whom some aspects of the sensory world are overwhelming and dysregulating. It is said that these individuals have a sensory processing disorder.

While the sensory gifts of being in nature help to foster optimal development and learning, being in nature and interacting with natural materials is also extremely helpful in calming and organizing a nervous system that is experiencing sensory challenges. When some children need additional sensory input, nature can provide everything they need.

Jameson was born prematurely. He was a fussy baby and grew into a toddler who was often called "quirky" and was said to "march to his own drummer." A highly sensitive child, he was easily upset and overwhelmed by his sensory world. Being in the presence of a group of children often overwhelmed him and resulted in the need for his parents to take him home early from birthday parties, sometimes before the presents were open and the cake was cut.

As Jameson grew older his challenges increased. He was diagnosed with anxiety, mood, and sensory-processing disorders. His parents consulted a variety of doctors and therapists and tried medication to help him. Nothing really seemed to work.

Jameson's family had a large backyard, and they spent a lot of time outside. It was not uncommon for Jameson to get in trouble for digging holes, lugging logs around the yard and leaving them strewn about, and making what he called "formulas" that consisted of stirring together mud, leaves, pine straw, rocks, and whatever else he could mix in a bucket with a bit of water.

After observing the ways in these sensory (heavy work) activities in nature helped foster a sense of calm and organization in Jameson, his parents stopped fussing at him for doing what he wanted and needed to do in the yard. The backyard became his sanctuary, and it was common for him to declare to his family at times when he was becoming overwhelmed and anxious that he was going outside to "chop some wood," "dig for treasures," or "build a tree house."

Note: At the time of this writing Jameson is a senior in high school and is reportedly applying to colleges that have natural resource and environmental science programs with a focus on forestry.

IMMUNE FUNCTIONING

The immune system is the body's defense against disease. This system has evolved from, in, and with nature. Separation from natural ecosystems—of which we are a part—can weaken our immune systems. This is due, in part, to a reduction of diversity in the systems' microbes. Homogeneity (having similarity) in microbes increases the risk of certain disorders, which can then lead to such health-related problems as diabetes, gastrointestinal disorders, and allergies (Roslund et al., 2020; Hanski et al., 2012).

Clemens Arvay, in *The Healing Code of Nature*, provides abundant evidence of ways in which contact with the nature environment contributes to our health, including the way in which microorganisms in our bodies keep our immune systems healthy. Certain aspects of our modern lifestyles, such as a high level of hygiene and reduced contact with nature, tend to reduce the diversity of such microorganisms. The solution offered by Arvay and many other researchers is to increase our active engagement with nature.

A few years ago, a multidisciplinary team of scholars (Frumkin et al., 2017) met to develop a plan for research into the connection between contact with nature and human health. They developed a list of twenty evidence-based health benefits of nature contact and suggested that there were likely many more. They also identified possible pathways through which nature contributes to human health; one such pathway was improved immune-system functioning. They determined from a review of related studies that early childhood exposure to particular microorganisms in the natural environment protects against certain diseases, especially allergic diseases, by contributing to the development of the immune system.

Natural environments rich in biodiversity help children develop a well-regulated immune system, as these environments contain a great variety and number of microscopic organisms. In Finland, researchers added forest-floor materials, sod, and planters of vegetables and flowers to child-care centers' play yards to see if increased contact with soil microorganisms affected children's immune systems (Puhakka et al., 2019). They found that children using the "greened" yards showed indications of improvements in their immune systems.

RESOURCES FOR GREEN SCHOOLYARDS

The green schoolyard initiative developed by the Children & Nature Network provides support and guidance for developing naturalized schoolyards throughout the country. Their Green Schoolyards Advocacy Toolkit is an excellent resource for rallying interest in green schoolyards and for providing information about how to start the process of transforming schoolyards into nature-rich environments. Learn more at https://www.childrenandnature.org/schools/greening-schoolyards/

Nature-Connecting Habitats for Children with Special Needs

Increased connectedness to nature is one of the desired outcomes of play and learning in natural environments. While the research on nature connections and children with special needs is somewhat scarce, interest in this area is growing. Findings generally report positive outcomes of efforts to increase connections between children with special needs and the world of nature. Yet, it's known that children with some forms of special needs generally participate less in outdoor play than their typically developing peers; and when they do play outdoors, their activities tend to be more restricted and disrupted than the play activities of other children (Galbraith and Lancaster, 2020; DaWalt et al., 2019).

In many cases, families and other caregivers are the gatekeepers of outdoor play for young children. They decide when, where, and how children will play outdoors. Their decisions are based on their understandings about the benefits of outdoor and nature-related play and on what they perceive as barriers and enablers for such play.

A study conducted in England investigated why families with children with special needs were generally absent in many spaces of play, leisure, and nature frequented by other families (Horton, 2017). Horton's research showed that, while physical barriers to accessibility sometimes deterred families from using the playspaces, negative emotional factors were greater deterrents. Physical barriers included inaccessible gates and entrances, trip hazards, and inaccessible toilets and other amenities. Social barriers included attitudes of other people, bullies, and limited experience of park staff in working with children with special needs. Families and caregivers described the emotional impacts of such barriers in terms of "dread" and "resignation." They reported a sense of failure in family engagement with outdoor and nature-related play. Most of the families and caregivers, however, also described moments of joy and quality time with their children at the parks.

Teachers, too, are decision makers about how and where children play. Their decisions can promote or limit children's independence and willingness to take risks. A study by researcher Julia Sterman and colleagues (2020) conducted with teachers and children in Sydney, Australia, investigated the effectiveness of promoting choice and control among children with special needs on the school playground. The goal of the intervention was to create increased independence and inclusion for all children on the playground. For this to occur, the school staff had to step back from their role as active supervisors and allow the children more control.

Families and educators discussed and learned about the benefits of engaging in manageable risk-taking and the consequences of preventing children from engaging in manageable risk-taking. As part of the study, researchers placed loose parts made of recycled materials with no obvious play value on the playground. The materials encouraged cooperative, gross-motor play and could be used in challenging, creative, and open-ended ways. Any hazards inherent to the materials could easily be identified and managed by a child. This intervention led to increased imaginative and social play on the part of the children and higher expectations of children's capabilities on the part of school staff.

This chapter has discussed ways in which time in natural environments can promote young children's play, learning, and quality of life. The next two chapters will zero in on specific elements often found in natural environments: chapter 9 on animals and chapter 10 on plants. Of course, children can interact with animals and plants in both outdoor and indoor settings. We will discuss ways of doing so, along with some safety-related guidelines.

REFERENCES

Brussoni, Mariana, et al. 2017. "Landscapes for Play: Effects of an Intervention to Promote Nature-Based Risky Play in Early Childhood Centres." *Journal of Environmental Psychology* 54: 139–150.

Chevalier, Gaétan, et al. 2012. "Earthing: Health Implications of Reconnecting the Human Body to the Earth's Surface Electrons." *Journal of Environmental and Public Health* 2012(3): 291541.

Cosco, Nilda, and Robin Moore. 2019. "Creating Inclusive Naturalized Outdoor Play Environments." In *Encyclopedia on Early Childhood Development* [online]. https://www.child-encyclopedia.com/outdoor-play/according-experts/creating-inclusive-naturalized-outdoor-play-environments

Cosco, Nilda, and Robin Moore. 2009. "Sensory Integration and Contact with Nature: Designing Outdoor Inclusive Environments." *North American Montessori Teachers Association Journal* 34(2): 158–177.

Cloward Drown, Kimberly, and Keith Christensen. 2014. "Dramatic Play Affordances of Natural and Manufactured Outdoor Settings for Preschool-Aged Children." *Children, Youth and Environments* 24(2): 53–77.

DaWalt, Leann S., et al. 2019. "Friendships and Social Participation as Markers of Quality of Life of Adolescents and Adults with Fragile X Syndrome and Autism." *Autism* 23(3): 383–393.

Frumkin, Howard, et al. 2017. "Nature Contact and Human Health: A Research Agenda." *Environmental Health Perspectives* 125(7). https://doi.org/10.1289/EHP1663

Galbraith, Carolyn, and Julie Lancaster. 2020. "Children with Autism in Wild Nature: Exploring Australian Parent Perceptions Using Photovoice." *Journal of Outdoor and Environmental Education* 23(3): 293–307.

Giusti, Matteo, et al. 2018. "A Framework to Assess Where and How Children Connect to Nature." *Frontiers in Psychology* 8: 2283.

Griffiths, Jay. 2013. *Kith: The Riddle of the Childscape.* London, UK: Hamish Hamilton Ltd.

Hanscom, Angela. 2016. *Balanced and Barefoot: How Unrestricted Outdoor Play Makes for Strong, Confident, and Capable Children.* Oakland, CA: New Harbinger Publications.

Hanski, Ilkka, et al. 2012. "Environmental Biodiversity, Human Microbiota, and Allergy Are Interrelated." *Proceedings of the National Academy of Sciences of the United States of America* 109(21): 8334–8339.

Horton, John. 2017. "Disabilities, Urban Natures, and Children's Outdoor Play." *Social and Cultural Geography* 18(8): 1152–1174.

Moore, Robin, and Nilda Cosco. 2007. "What Makes a Park Inclusive and Universally Designed? A Multi-Method Approach." In *Open Space People Space.* London, UK: Taylor and Francis.

Moore, Robin, Susan Goltsman, and Daniel Iacofano, eds. 1992. *Play for All Guidelines: Planning, Design, and Management of Outdoor Play Settings for All Children.* 2nd ed. Berkeley, CA: MIG Communications.

Puhakka, Riikka, et al. 2019. "Greening of Daycare Yards with Biodiverse Materials Affords Well-Being, Play, And Environmental Relationships." *International Journal of Environmental Research and Public Health* 16(16): 2948.

Roslund, Marja I., et al. 2020. "Biodiversity Intervention Enhances Immune Regulation and Health-Associated Commensal Microbiota among Daycare Children." *Science Advances* 6(42). doi:10.1126/sciadv.aba2578

Sterman, Julia, et al. 2020. "Creating Play Opportunities on the School Playground: Educator Experiences of the Sydney Playground Project." *Australian Occupational Therapy Journal* 67(1): 62–73.

CHAPTER 9

Connecting
with Animals

"

Animals make us human.

— **TEMPLE GRANDIN,**
scientist and activist

Connection to nature is sometimes defined as the way in which people identify with the natural world and the relationships they form with elements in the natural world, such as plants and animals. Children's connections with nature are influenced by their enjoyment of nature, empathy for creatures, sense of oneness, and sense of responsibility.

Animals and Children's Connection to Nature

Some of the research on connectedness to nature focuses specifically on preschool-age children and their interactions with animals. David Sobel, for example, identified "developing friendships with animals" as a universal play motif with young children (Sobel, 2008). Along similar lines, Peter Kahn and his colleagues identified "cohabiting with a wild animal" as one of the keystone interaction patterns exhibited by preschool children at a nature preschool (Kahn, Weiss, and Harrington, 2018). The "wild animals" in this case were not elephants and tigers but such common backyard animals as birds, spiders, and worms. Another researcher, Matteo Giusti, identified "involvement with animals" as one of the key experiences that influence children's connection to nature (Giusti, 2018). Giusti's work focuses on developing environments for children that help them connect to nature. He refers to such environments as "nature-connecting habitats" for children, and he identified the presence of animals as an integral part of such environments. Giusti emphasizes the importance of children learning to be not only *in* and *for* nature but also *with* nature. Being in an animal's presence—and being present to the animal—may be one of the most memorable experiences a child can have of being with nature.

Let's take a look at three of the keystone interaction patterns identified by Kahn and his colleagues about preschool children and animals: cohabiting with animals, observing animals, and imitating animals.

COHABITING WITH ANIMALS

Kahn and his coresearchers offer an example of *cohabiting*—living in the same space or existing together— with animals involving two preschool children and an earthworm. One boy, while pushing a wheelbarrow, came close to running over an earthworm but stopped just in time to avoid hitting it. An observant teacher noticed what was going on. She picked up the worm and placed it in her hand. She showed it to a girl who was also watching the earthworm scenario. This child, while at first showing some aversion to the worm, was soon fascinated by it. The boy with the wheelbarrow carefully removed the worm from the teacher's hand and placed it some feet away from his construction zone to keep the worm safe. In this instance, both children were cohabiting with the worm. The one child, by just being in its company; the other, by placing it in a safe place. The teacher played an important role in the process by attending to what the children were experiencing.

This earthworm scenario was an unplanned happening with wildlife, but adults can also plan encounters with wild animals. Some schools are setting the stage for this by transforming barren grounds into nature-rich environments that invite wildlife. As discussed in chapter 8, these environments include naturalized playspaces and green schoolyards featuring natural elements such as trees, bushes, gardens, rocks, and other natural materials. Environments might also include specific invitations for wildlife, such as butterfly gardens, bird feeders, and "mini-beast" areas where snails, spiders, earwigs, and other small creatures can thrive. Some schools have even established beehives. A related research study showed that being in the presence of bees prompted a shift in elementary children from fear of bees to fascination and appreciation (Cho and Lee, 2018). Another study looked at how

young children develop understanding and empathy through cohabiting with animals. Nxumalo (2017) focused on changes in preschool children's attitudes and behaviors after a teacher called the children's attention to the fact that the apple tree in the playground had not flowered that spring and that there were few bees on the playground. The bees that were present were either dead or moving slowly on the ground. After learning that the bumblebees in the yard are generally not aggressive unless threatened, the children became more comfortable being close to the bees and cohabiting with them. They started practicing stillness and moving slowly while close to bees still showing signs of life. Some children offered flowers and sugary water to the bees. They touched the wings and soft "fur" of dead bees and provided covering to keep them from blowing away. The children's encounters with the bees helped them develop ecological perspective taking and gave them opportunities to practice empathy.

COHABITING WITH ANIMALS
BIRDS

Materials

- ✿ Heavy-duty plant pot with saucer
- ✿ Water
- ✿ Small rock
- ✿ Popcorn, berries, citrus slices
- ✿ String
- ✿ Plastic needle
- ✿ Scissors

What to Do

✿ Place the pot, upside down, near a bush and away from active play areas. Birds are more likely to use the bath if it's in a more secluded area of the yard.

✿ Place the saucer on top of the pot.

✿ Fill the saucer with water.

✿ Place a small rock in the middle of the saucer.

✿ Involve the children in keeping the bird bath clean and filled with water.

✿ Attract birds to the play yard by threading popcorn, berries, and/or citrus slices onto a long piece of string.

✿ Hang the food onto branches for the birds to eat.

✿ You can set out short pieces of string in the yard for the birds to use in making their nests.

Cohabiting with an animal may be especially helpful for children with special needs. Animals are nonjudgmental and make fewer demands than humans. An animal accepts a child as he or she is. The animal doesn't ask the child to conform to any standards of what is "normal." This acceptance can be comforting and calming for children who struggle with many demands of daily life. Engaging children with special needs in the care of animals can also foster their sense of efficacy and self-esteem.

OBSERVING ANIMALS

"Looking at wild animals" is another of the keystone interaction patterns identified by Kahn and his colleagues. There's a tendency to draw others into what we find fascinating in our observations of animals. I witnessed this phenomenon involving a three-year-old child with autism. While this example relates to a baby chick instead of a wild animal, it illustrates the potential benefits of children observing animals.

> I arrived at a preschool classroom early one morning in November. A mother and her three-year-old daughter with autism arrived at about the same time. While the mother stopped to talk to the teacher, the child walked over to a table where eggs had been incubating for the past several weeks. The child noticed a chick starting to peck its way out of an egg. The girl ran back to her mother, grabbed her arm, and pointed. She said, "Look!" This was the first word the child had spoken in the classroom since she had begun attending that school three months earlier. The child also made eye contact with her mother during this interaction. That, too, was unusual, as making eye contact was something her mother rarely witnessed, even at home.

IMITATING ANIMALS

Kahn and his colleagues (2018) identified "imitating animals" as another of the keystone interaction patterns of children interacting with nature. They describe one young girl imitating the physical actions and vocalizations of a domestic housecat. They note how the child makes eye contact with a peer as she pretends to be a cat. She seems to be inviting another child to become a part of the play scenario.

Other researchers describe a group of young children in Australia imitating animals (Taylor and Pacini-Ketchabaw, 2016). This time, the animals involved were large mobs of kangaroos living in the grasslands near the child-care center. The children showed a strong interest in being close to the kangaroos. While there was some hesitancy at first, they gradually became increasingly confident in getting closer and closer to the animals. As the children got closer and spent more time near the kangaroos, they noticed how they and the kangaroos were alike in some ways but also different. The children started to experiment with what it would be like to live in a kangaroo's body. They found materials to make big tails, attached them to their bodies, and hopped around. They put their hands on their heads to mimic the action of the protruding swiveling ears. At one point, they even pretended to be dead and dying kangaroos.

Children may not be able to explain why they imitate animals, but this behavior occurs often enough and spontaneous enough to understand why it's considered a universal play motif. Becoming an animal in play may reflect a connection or relationship that neither we nor children can clearly put into words. Perhaps *kinship* is the closest we can come to explaining this phenomenon.

COHABITING WITH ANIMALS
IMITATING

You can use a modified form of yoga to encourage children to imitate animals. Before doing this activity, engage the children in looking at photos or videos depicting how different animals stand and move. Also, encourage them to choose backyard animals for their yoga poses. For children who have balance problems, place them next to a wall or piece of heavy furniture that they can hold onto.

You might start by having the children do the cobra pose.

What to Do

- ❁ Lie facedown on the floor with tops of your feet flat on the floor.
- ❁ Keep your arms close to your body as you place your palms down on the floor near your chest.
- ❁ Extend your arms to lift the front of your body from the floor.
- ❁ Have the children take turns demonstrating how different animals stand and move.

Animals' Effects on Social Interactions, Stress, and Social-Emotional Development

Animals are sometimes referred to as "social lubricants" because they can promote social interactions. Research shows that this social-lubricant factor can be effective in helping children with ASD interact more with peers and adults. One study investigated the effects of a classroom-based animal-assisted activities (AAA) program with guinea pigs on the social functioning of primary school children (O'Haire et al., 2013). Results showed that children with ASD talked more to people, looked more at faces of people, and made more physical contact with humans in the presence of two guinea pigs. They also displayed more positive affect (such as smiling and laughing) and less negative affect (such as frowning and whining). The researchers did not observe increases in these behaviors when the children interacted with a selection of age-appropriate toys. The children with ASD also received more positive social approaches from their peers when the animals were involved.

Some children with ASD demonstrate visual abnormalities, such as failing to make eye contact and to look at someone in social situations, which seem to be associated with an overall reduced inclination to interact socially. They also may demonstrate less pointing, showing objects, orienting to their name, social smiling, shared affect (sharing emotions and recognizing emotions in others), and social vocalizations. This phenomenon may be due to neurobiological deficits in recognizing these interactions as rewarding. It may also reflect anxiety, a common characteristic of people with ASD. The presence of an animal can reduce social anxiety and prompt more positive social interactions (O'Haire et al., 2013) because an animal's presence can make people and situations seem less threatening.

Animals tend to have a stress-reducing effect on people. Some researchers suggest that humans have an innate tendency toward biophilia—to focus on life and lifelike processes (Wilson, 1984). There are some indications that animals play a special role in activating our biophilia forces (Arvay, 2018), which may then lead to a reduction in stress. The idea of animals as social facilitators supports the use of animals in therapeutic programs (Valiyamattam et al., 2020), as well as in other intervention and educational settings, including classrooms and homes. Of course, the presence of animals can support the development of typically developing children, as well as children with special needs.

Patty Born Selly, in *Connecting Animals and Children in Early Childhood*, discusses how animals can promote all areas of development, including social-emotional, cognitive, physical, and ecological. Selly states how the relationships, nuances, and engagements between child and animal are themselves teachers. She encourages educators and other adults working with children to recognize ways in which an animal and a child become equal partners in cocreating an experience. While Selly recognizes the importance of learning about and for animals, she also emphasizes the value of learning *with* animals, which means viewing animals as partners in the experience and recognizing them as members of a community of nature.

Dr. Selly also notes that, while domesticated animals can promote children's development, encounters with wild animals tend to offer "something extra-special." Encounters with common creatures such as butterflies, squirrels, and birds in their natural habitats can be exciting and meaningful for young children. Observing animals in their natural habitats helps children realize that animals—like themselves—have homes. While animal homes differ from ours, children find it fascinating that animal homes are generally built by the animals themselves. Selly notes that children are also fascinated by the fact that many wild animals have "special powers"—some fly, some live underground, and some hibernate for months at a time. She uses the term *zoomorphism* to describe children's playacting at being animals (Selly, 2014), such as by making animal noises, moving like animals, or saying things they wish an animal would say. According to Dr. Selly, these zoomorphic behaviors reflect children's attempt to internalize their understandings about animals, reflect children's acceptance of animals as individuals, and the children's ability—or attempts—to take the perspective of another creature.

Richard Louv, in *Our Wild Calling*, also speaks to the special qualities of engagement with wild animals. He describes what many of us experience when in the presence of a wild animal: a shift in our experience of time and space. Louv describes a disappearance of a separate "me and you" or "me and nature." What remains is the relationship. Children, too—or maybe even especially—can experience and benefit from such encounters.

A recent study shows that children are easily fascinated by and enjoy hands-on experiences (Lerstrup, Chawla, and Heft, in press) with small creatures such as insects, worms, snails, and frogs. The study focused primarily on how young children's engagement with small creatures might promote the development of care toward the natural world. This study also sought to identify the kind of activities preschool children perform with small creatures and what the children might gain from their acquaintance with these creatures. Findings showed that children experienced attraction, excitement, fascination, and joy. The children also developed understandings about animals and ecosystems and about life processes and interconnectedness. Additionally, they developed a caring attitude towards small creatures and the places where they live.

We know that not all children have frequent opportunities to observe or interact with animals, especially animals that aren't pets. They may not even be aware of the fact that different forms of wild animals live right outside their door. I once asked preschool children if they thought they could find wildlife in their backyard or neighborhood. Most of the children answered with a definite no. One child told me that was a "silly question."

We should take children's unfamiliarity with common wild animals seriously. The benefits of young children engaging with animals are too great to be dismissed, especially for children with ASD and other types of special needs.

Animal-Assisted Therapy

Educational professionals have used a variety of animals (horses, dogs, cats, birds, guinea pigs, and farm animals) effectively in therapeutic programs, with horses being the most common. Using an animal to enhance or complement traditional therapy is called animal-assisted therapy (AAT). Some physicians are suggesting therapy dogs or companion animals for children with ADHD and other areas of special needs. For children with autism, AAT can increase social interaction and communication skills and decrease ASD symptom severity, stress, and problem behaviors (Valiyamattam et al, 2020). The presence of animals is associated with healthy changes in the concentration of certain neurotransmitters, such as the "happy hormone" dopamine and the natural painkiller endorphin (Arvay, 2018).

A recent study compared the visual attention to animal and human faces in children with ASD and typically developing children (Valiyamattam et al. 2020). Not surprisingly, the typically developing children showed significantly greater social attention to both human and animal faces than the children with ASD. However, the children with ASD showed significantly greater attention to animal faces than to human faces. This study suggests that children with ASD may experience greater social rewards and less social anxiety in the presence of animals than in the presence of humans. These findings add to the strong evidence base for the use of animal-assisted interventions for children with autism.

COHABITING WITH ANIMALS
BUG BOX

Materials

- ❀ Clear plastic container
- ❀ Dish soap
- ❀ Water
- ❀ Sponge
- ❀ Hammer
- ❀ Nail

- ❀ Small creatures*, such as snails, crickets, worms, ladybugs
- ❀ Leaves, twigs, other natural materials**

*Avoid animals that may bite or sting.
**Avoid plants that may cause skin irritation or allergic reactions.

What to Do

- ✿ Clean the container thoroughly with soap and water, making sure to remove any food, detergents, or other substances that may be harmful to a living creature. Let dry.

- ✿ Punch small holes in the top and/or sides of the container so that the animals can breathe.

- ✿ Collect one or several critters, such as snails, crickets, worms, or ladybugs.

- ✿ Add leaves, twigs, or other natural materials to provide an appropriate habitat for the animal.

Invite the children to observe the animals. Be mindful that some children may be afraid of bugs or have an aversion to being close to bugs. Encourage close observation, but avoid pushing a child into uncomfortable situations.

After observing the animals for a short period of time (no more than a few days), put them back where you found them.

Promoting Connections
between Children and Animals

The many benefits of connecting children with animals invite some thought as to what families, teachers, and other adults can do to promote positive interactions. Here are some ideas.

- **Spend time outdoors looking for animals and signs of animals.** Try to discover where the animals live. Look for nests and burrows. Look under logs and rocks. Remember, you might hear a bird before you see it. You might not see a deer or a squirrel, but you might find its tracks in the mud, sand, or snow. Look for clues about what the animals eat. Can you find partially eaten leaves or teeth marks on the bark of a tree? Provide observational tools, such as magnifiers, hand lenses, children's binoculars, and simple guidebooks to invite closer observation. **Hint:** Some animals may be hard to spot because of their small size, camouflage, or shyness, and some children may not have the patience or ability to wait for an animal to make itself known. One technique you can use to make animals more visible is to shake them out of a bush. Place a large piece of white or light-colored cloth on the ground under a bush. Gently shake the branches or leaves of the bush, and watch as the small creatures drop onto the cloth.

- **Provide props for animal costumes and imitation of animal behaviors.** You might use fake fur, masks, or homemade wings or beaks. Provide a variety of natural materials for making nests and dens. **Hint:** Some children may assume the role of aggressive or threatening animals. Guide their enthusiasm by running across the yard with them or presenting physical challenges for them to overcome, such as overturning a log or large rock.

- **Involve children in the care of animals.** Encourage children to think about what an animal needs, such as food, water, shelter, and so on. Ask them what an animal may be feeling: afraid, safe, excited, warm, cold. It's okay if children use *anthropomorphism*—attributing human characteristics and/or behaviors to other-than-human entities—in talking about animals. Anthropomorphism can make animals more relatable and can help children better understand or empathize with animals (Chawla, 2009). The most important thing is that children show respect for the animals. Encouraging a child to think about what an animal needs or is experiencing may be especially meaningful for a child with autism. Children on the autism spectrum often have difficulty interpreting intent behind human actions; interpreting intent is sometimes easier with an animal. A horse reaching for an apple, for example, is a likely indication that the horse wants to eat. A dog rolling over on its back is an invitation for a belly rub.

- **Be selective in the language you use in reference to animals.** Referring to an animal as a *pest* does little to foster a positive attitude toward that animal, but referring to an animal as a *friend* or *neighbor* tends to do the opposite. **Hint:** Encourage children to name an animal that they see on a regular basis. A name based on some special characteristic or behavior of the animal can be especially meaningful. For example, Nutty or Bushy Tail might be a good name for a squirrel that hangs out near the playspace.

✿ **Foster empathy by engaging the imagination.** You might do this through storytelling, role-playing, and mimicry. Kahn and his colleagues (2016) identified engaging the imagination as one of the keystone interaction patterns and described this as "imagining nature to be something other than it is." They give an example of a child using a stick as something to ride. At first, it's a "train" but later becomes a "horse." Use "wondering" statements to engage children's imaginations about animals; for example, statements such as, "I wonder why Nutty the squirrel keeps flicking its tail," invite children to consider more closely what the squirrel is experiencing or trying to communicate. You can also invite wondering questions from the children by asking, "What do you wonder about?"

✿ **Encourage the children to draw pictures of animals or use clay to sculpt an animal.** This process draws attention to the physical characteristics of the animal— the shape of its ears, the length of its tail, the placement of its eyes, and so on. Avoid displaying cartoonish depictions of animals. Use photos or drawings of real animals, and provide books with realistic depictions of animals. **Hint:** Some children with autism and other special needs may have difficulty with fine-motor activities such as drawing and sculpting. You can make tools, such as crayons, pencils, and paintbrushes, easier for a child to grasp and manipulate. For example, lengthen or shorten the handle on a paintbrush. Build up a handle with chenille stems, or attach the handle to the child's hand using a Velcro strap. You can give large crayons to children who have difficulty holding on to small items or build up regular-size pencils and crayons with masking tape. To keep drawing paper from shifting around, tape it to a table. For painting on an easel, you can use tape or paper clips to hold the paper in place.

COHABITING WITH ANIMALS
HEALTH

Direct contact with animals carries a small risk of certain diseases, particularly with very young children. Minimize these risks by consistently taking the following steps:

- Keep animals and animal-care products away from food-preparation or eating areas.
- Wash hands with soap and water immediately (or as soon as possible) after handling or visiting animals.
- Use paper towels or other towels that are not shared for drying hands.

Additional information is available through the Pet Care Trust (https://www.petsintheclassroom.org/preventing-disease-transmission/) and the Centers for Disease Control (https://www.cdc.gov/healthypets/specific-groups/schools.html)

- **Promote an appreciation of birds by encouraging children to build a bird's nest.** Start by calling attention to what a real bird's nest looks like, with either a real nest or photos. Engage the children in making a list of materials needed for building a nest, such as small twigs and other plant parts, mud, and so on. Gather the materials and invite nest building. If you find an abandoned bird's nest, you can put it in a plastic bag or other clear plastic container for close observation. To protect the children from possible parasites, avoid having them actually handle a real nest. **Hint:** You may wish to confine the nest building to a small paper bowl. This may reduce children's frustration with holding the materials together.

- **Invite a trainer of support animals or a person who uses a support animal to visit your classroom.** Encourage the visitor to give clear guidelines about how the children should relate to the animal. Also, inform the visitor about the special needs of individual children in the classroom.

- **Invite wildlife to the play yard by providing habitat.** Rotting logs, wooden pallets, a piece of wet carpet, or cardboard squares in a secluded spot will invite a variety of mini beasts. Establish other wildlife habitats—such as butterfly gardens and bird feeders—near classroom windows. If windows are too high, provide a platform for observation. See chapter 8 for additional ideas on how to attract wildlife through the development of an environmental yard.

- **Invite families of children with special needs to bring their pets to school.** This activity may be especially rewarding for a child with special needs, as the pet and the child will already be comfortable with each other. Be sure to check with classroom families in advance regarding any concerns about allergies or fears. Also, set guidelines as to how the children should relate to the visiting animal.

- **Add replicas of animals to indoor and outdoor play areas.** Pay attention to the quality and size of the animal replicas, and try to add realistic depictions. Also consider habitat—a giraffe in a farm setting, for example, isn't appropriate.

- **Plan trips to places featuring animals, such as farms, ranches, nature preserves, zoos, and aquariums.** Before a field trip with children with special needs, consider the following:
  - What mobility challenges might a child face?
  - Will the change in location and schedule make some children feel overly anxious?
  - How can I prepare the child for this new experience?
  - Is extra adult support needed?
  - Will pairing each child with a partner be helpful?

Knowing Animals as Kin

Positive interactions with animals make important contributions to a child's quality of life, yet many children today have only limited opportunities for deep engagement with animals. We, as adults, can help young children experience a life that is "really good" by strengthening their connections with animals and other living things.

Many of us focus on fostering wonder as we work with children. We view wonder as a unifying context in children's explorations, discoveries, imaginings, and ponderings related to the natural world. We want children to experience the natural world as a place of wonder.

We can foster young children's sense of wonder in a number of ways, but perhaps the most effective is to encourage a deep sense of kinship with nature. Wonder is important, but wonder without a sense of kinship isn't enough. An overemphasis on scientific ways of knowing can reinforce the concept that nature is something separate from humans and something to be manipulated and controlled. Viewing the natural world through the eyes of wonder calls for rich sensory experiences with the world of nature, as well as going beyond scientific knowing to include compassion, generosity, vulnerability, openness, empathy, and respect for otherness. Connecting children with animals can promote such dispositions.

Patty Born Selly offers the following reflection on the interdependence between children and animals.

Many early care and education providers are attracted to the idea of animal-assisted therapies or classroom support animals for children with special needs. In this context, animals can be important coaches or tools in helping children to grow, develop, and interact successfully with others. Sometimes they can do things for children that children cannot physically do on their own, and this is literally life-changing for children. In such cases, the purpose or "job" of the animal is clear: to be a supporter to children and to work in service of the children's emotional or physical needs.

There are additional nuances to child-animal relationships that warrant consideration as well, beyond the service or "helper" role. We could regard animals not just for what they do for children, but through the lens of a reciprocal relationship, what Oliver (2016) calls "interspecies interdependence." What if in supporting child-animal relations we help animals as much as they help us?

The inclusion of injured, rehabilitated, "nonreleasable," or rescue animals is a relatively common practice in nature-based preschool settings that aim to deepen children's relationships to and empathy for nature. This can be an important way to support the relationship between children and animals. In these interactions, the child is not dependent on the animal for success; instead, the children and animals share an interdependence that is more equitable. There are multiple ways in which these relationships of interspecies independence may be beneficial to all children. First, by giving children an active role in the care and keeping of the animal, this approach ensures that children will develop sensitivity and awareness to the unique needs, situation, and experiences of the animal. Numerous research studies assert the connection between caring for animals and the development of empathy and perspective-taking. For example, a nature preschool was home to a wood duck that had imprinted on humans as a hatchling and was, therefore, deemed unreleasable. The children in the preschool visited him each day, talked and interacted with him, and actively showed a concern for his well-being through monitoring his food and water intake, ensuring he had enough outside time every day, and speculating about his experience. Clearly, they considered him to be a very important part of their preschool community and looked after him with great care.

Additionally, caring for and housing animals with physical impairments, such as broken wings or permanent injuries, may also help to normalize physical disability, since the disability is something the children see and deal with on an everyday basis. Actively involving children in caring for animals in these situations means that they will be exposed to any number of physical limitations and will allow them to see the animals' adaptations to those limitations, their vulnerabilities, and their resilience. Although research in this area is scant, it is reasonable to think that making animals with impairments a part of the community may support children in their understanding and acceptance of others who have physical or cognitive limitations. In doing this, the adults assert that these animals are just an everyday part of the children's experience. The children's relationship is not based on the animal's limitations. Shifting the focus away from the limitations and instead on the relationship is a way of supporting the multispecies connection.

I am a former wildlife rehabilitator and have been caring for an unreleasable box turtle for many years. She was struck by a car and as a result her two back legs were crushed and had to be amputated. When children meet her for the first time, they sometimes remark about her lack of legs or ask questions about how she gets around, but for the most part, they are quite matter-of-fact about her disability.

I have introduced children to raptors and other birds with permanent injuries, including a Cooper's hawk who suffered a broken wing, which hung limply at his side. The children occasionally had questions about how he managed to fly (he couldn't) and how he caught his prey (it was delivered to him every morning), but their focus was on constructing their knowledge of him, on understanding his experience and his relationship with his environment. Their focus was on how they could relate to him. These examples offer evidence that children are quite capable of looking beyond physical limitations or disabilities. Opportunities to connect to animals in caring, interspecies, interdependent relationships may well support children's innate desire for inclusion of their peers with disabilities or other limitations.

In the next chapter, we'll take a look at ways to connect with plants in nature.

REFERENCES

Arvay, Clemens G. 2018. *The Healing Code of Nature.* Boulder, CO: Sounds True.

Born, Patty. 2018. "Regarding Animals: A Perspective on the Importance of Animals in Early Childhood Environmental Education." *International Journal of Early Childhood Environmental Education* 5(2): 46–57.

Chawla, Louise. 2009. "Growing Up Green: Becoming an Agent of Care for the Natural World." *Journal of Developmental Processes* 4(1): 6–23.

Cho, Yoori, and Dowon Lee. 2017. "'Love Honey, Hate Honey Bees': Reviving Biophilia of Elementary School Students through Environmental Education Program." *Environmental Education Research* 24(3): 1–16.

Giusti, Matteo, et al. 2018. "A Framework to Assess Where and How Children Connect to Nature." *Frontiers in Psychology* 8: 2283.

Kahn, Peter H., Thea Weiss, and Kit Harrington. 2018. "Modeling Child-Nature Interaction in a Nature Preschool: A Proof of Concept." *Frontiers in Psychology* 9: 835.

Lerstrup, Inger, Louise Chawla, and Harry Heft. In press. "Affordances of Small Animals for Young Children: A Path to Environmental Values of Care." *International Journal of Early Childhood Environmental Education.*

Nxumalo, Fikile. 2017. "Stories for Living on a Damaged Planet: Environmental Education in a Preschool Classroom." *Journal of Early Childhood Research* 16(2): 148–159.

O'Haire, Marguerite, et al. 2013. "Effects of Animal-Assisted Activities with Guinea Pigs in the Primary School Classroom." *Anthrozoös* 26(3): 445–458.

Oliver, Kelly. 2016. "Service Dogs: Between Animal Studies and Disability Studies." *philoSOPHIA* 6(2): 241–258. doi:10.1353/phi.2016.0021

Selly, Patty Born. 2014. *Connecting Animals and Children in Early Childhood.* St. Paul, MN: Redleaf.

Sobel, David. 2008. *Childhood and Nature: Design Principles for Educators.* Portland, ME: Stenhouse.

Taylor, Affrica, Veronica Pacini-Ketchabaw. 2016. "Kids, Raccoons, and Roos: Awkward Encounters and Mixed Affects." *Children's Geographies* 15(2): 131–145.

Valiyamattam, Georgitta J., et al. 2020. "Do Animals Engage Greater Social Attention in Autism? An Eye Tracking Analysis." *Frontiers in Psychology* 11: 727.

Wilson, Edward O. 1984. *Biophilia.* Cambridge, MA: Harvard University Press.

CHAPTER 10

Connecting with Plants

"

Plants remind us
to move in nature time.

— RUTH WILSON

Plants play a critical role in sustaining life on earth, including the lives of humans. Their importance to human functioning, however, is sometimes overlooked. Plants give us food and oxygen and so much more. Many of the medicines we take to ease pain and cure or prevent physical illness originally came from plants. The benefits we get from plants, however, aren't confined to just our physical bodies. The presence of plants and engagement with plants benefit our minds and spirits as well. This chapter will discuss ways in which these benefits apply to children with varying abilities.

☀ The Power of Plants

Young children seem to know intuitively that plants are good for us. In one study, three- to five-year-old children were asked to explain how they experience relaxation (Cooke et al., 2020). Many of the children described how such experiences often occur in nature-rich environments. They explained how watching and touching natural elements helped them feel relaxed. Just looking at trees and lying in the soft grass made them feel happy and relaxed. These findings are consistent with other studies in which children described how observing beauty in natural landscapes helped them cope with stressful situations (Arvidsen and Beames, 2019).

Children with ASD and ADHD tend to experience more troublesome anxiety conditions than other children. Their anxiety is sometimes expressed by increased aggression, conduct problems, depression, self-injury, insistence on sameness, and irritability. Exposure to plant-rich environments may lower children's stress and anxiety and potentially minimize some of the associated problematic behaviors (Bratman et al., 2015). Some research shows that children with ADHD who regularly play in green settings have milder ADHD symptoms than children who play in built outdoor and indoor settings (Faber Taylor and Kuo, 2011).

At times, experiencing a close connection with just a single plant can break the emotionally locked state a child might be experiencing. This occurred one day with a four-year-old child who, after demonstrating aggressive behaviors in the preschool classroom, was brought to the director's office. She threw chairs, hit and kicked, and spit in the director's face. A bit of the spittle landed on a plant. The director responded by calmly wiping the spittle from her face and then turned to the child and said, "Would you like to wipe the spit off of the plant? I'm worried that it might make the plant sick." The child took a tissue and gently removed the saliva from the leaves of the plant. She seemed more concerned than angry. The director asked the child if she would like to sit with her for a while. The child crawled into the director's lap and questioned her about the plant. The child asked if the plant would die, if it might be sad, and what they could do to make it better. After watering the plant and even talking to it a bit, the child went back to her classroom and was fine the rest of the day. Focusing on a plant and caring for it during a time of emotional pain seemed to calm the child. Caring for something outside herself—and something she may have hurt—seemed to be healing for this child.

Rachel Tenney, an early childhood special-education teacher, describes another example of the power of plants:

Ralph struggled with emotional outbursts long before I met him. His challenging behaviors in preschool almost led to his removal, before I was placed with him midyear. And his continuation in the program was precarious. Could I, as a special-education teacher, support him in a way that would keep everyone safe? Could he respond to yet another intervention in an environment that asked a lot of him?

After several weeks, the preschool teachers were trusting me more. We began to notice some predictability in Ralph's behaviors and altered our expectations to meet his level of functioning. During a weekly meeting with the teachers, I shared with them my interest in taking care of street trees. In Brooklyn, we are lucky to have thousands of trees, called *street trees*, planted by the parks department. The task of taking care of the trees often falls on neighbors and volunteers. The teachers invited me to share some of my knowledge about trees with the class, as they prepared to adopt a tree by the school.

To our surprise, Ralph already knew that street trees needed to be watered and that dog waste could be harmful to them. During an outing to look at street trees, he shared some observations about trees that were in good shape and trees that needed our help. After the outing, Ralph—who generally avoided drawing due to his perfectionist streak and poor fine-motor control—chose to draw a picture of a tree!

As our walks that spring stretched farther from the classroom and up into the big park, Ralph and I would talk about trees as we passed. He came to recognize the most familiar ones: London planetree and *Ginkgo biloba*. Even as he tired from the long uphill trip, Ralph remained interested in the surroundings and avoided negative interactions with his classmates. At the park, he gradually became more confident in his interactions with others and started to engage in pretend play with his classmates. In the classroom, play with others often led to conflicts about toys or materials or what roles each child would take. But outdoors, Ralph's respect for his classmates' boundaries was evident, and he could independently play for long stretches of time without my intervention.

As the year drew to a close, Ralph had the opportunity to choose a reward for making positive choices. He chose street-tree care time. In preparation for a street-tree outing, Ralph carefully traced letters for a sign that read "No Dog Poop" in English and Hebrew. This was something he thought of on his own. On our appointed afternoon, Ralph diligently removed ivy and cultivated the small tree pit for the London planetree in front of the building where he lived. He proudly placed the sign he had lettered. He remained focused for more than two hours caring for multiple trees on his block. I had never seen this depth of focused attention from him before. He wanted to keep going, but we had to stop for his dinnertime.

As the year ended, I reflected on the progress Ralph had made and realized how our time with trees and in the park helped us both weather a difficult time and emerge as partners in the growth process. I've continued to see Ralph over the years since his preschool days. We continue to take care of trees along his block. Ralph now attends a school for students with multiple special educational needs. Our talks, whenever we're together, tend to focus on nature and concerns about climate change.

※※

What Plants and Trees Offer Children

Most young children like to do more than just look at plants and trees. They want to engage with plants. They want to plant seeds, pick flowers, climb trees, and use branches to build a fort. Children tend to view plants as more than an "it" to be viewed, used, or admired, a perspective that seems to apply especially to their engagement with trees. Some children look to trees as friends and even hold conversations with them.

One research study reported an incident of young children discovering "baby trees" during their walk through a forest (Argent et al., 2017). The children stopped to "sing familiar songs softly and whisper words of encouragement." They wondered about the trees having a heart and were concerned about how the trees felt when they were being taken down for a land development project. The children's relationship with the trees was based more on an attitude of "What can I do for the trees?" than "What can the trees do for me?" They expressed care for the trees without any expectation of reward or positive outcome for themselves. The children weren't relating to nature as something to control; they were just seeing nature as a place to be, to hang out with, and play with as a friend.

In another study, a child talked about missing trees (Zimanyi and Rossovska, 2020) after moving on from a forest preschool to a traditional public-school kindergarten. During one of the first days of outdoor playtime at the public school, this child asked, "Where are all the trees?" Sadly, there was not a single tree on the playground.

One reason why children enjoy trees and other plants relates to what these organisms offer children for play and exploration. Trees invite climbing. Downed branches and sticks invite den building. Seeds and leaves invite collecting and sorting. Plant parts invite imaginary cooking and creative collages. We see from just these few examples that plants and plant parts tend to invite different types of play: constructive, sociodramatic, creative, risky, and so on. In the following vignette, Jennifer Rosinia describes the positive influence of trees on her children's childhood:

One of the biggest reasons why we bought the house was because there was an open lot behind it as well as one to the north. The house came with a big fenced-in yard, and when combined with the open lots, the sight line was beautiful with large trees, flowers, and a neighbor's vegetable garden.

About a year after we bought the house, we learned that the open lot behind us had been sold. It was heartbreaking to watch the trees being cut down. And when the new neighbors built a second garage, the sight line was gone. Three children later, we learned that the lot to the north was up for sale. The children loved playing on that lot, climbing the trees and allowing their imaginations run wild. If/when that lot sold, the new owner would most likely cut the trees down. Saving them and preserving an open space for our children to play became a priority. We did what we had to do in order to purchase that property.

Those trees became a gathering place for all the children in the neighborhood. On any given day, the nature space was transformed through the children's creativity and found items into a café, a bookstore, a campsite, a kitchen, and a variety of houses. Children read books while sitting high up in the trees. They shared picnic lunches during the summer months and enjoyed many gallons of hot chocolate while building huge hills and snow people. The children are grown now, but the trees remain, as do the memories.

While plants and trees are enjoyed by all children, they may be especially helpful for children with autism. In one study of an intervention program in Sweden for children with autism and severe delays in speech and language development, researchers found that the program was effective in reducing children's stress, awakening their curiosity and interest, prompting spontaneous attention, and vitalizing energy (Byström, Grahn, and Hägerhäll, 2019). Researchers attributed some of these positive outcomes—especially decreased stress and increased vitality—to the soft and repetitive movements occurring in nature, such as the tree canopy swaying softly in the wind. At times, such movements elicited joint attention between a child and the therapist.

Joint attention—sometimes referred to as shared attention—is the shared focus of two or more individuals on an object or situation of interest. Joint attention often occurs when one person alerts another to an object or situation by means of eye-gazing, pointing, or other verbal or nonverbal indications. Impairments in joint attention are among the earliest signs of autism, and the development of joint-attention skills one of the high-priority goals of early intervention for children with ASD (Byström, Grahn, and Hägerhäll, 2019). The fact that certain movement dynamics of nature elicited joint attention for the children in the farm-based intervention program described on page 136 was significant. Priorities of the program included promoting social and language skills, and joint attention is known to play a critical role in the development of these skills. Other research supports the positive effects of plants and trees in nature-based therapies for children with ADHD by improving their on-task behavior and decreasing their behavioral problems (Swank and Smith-Adcock, 2018).

Several of the keystone interaction patterns identified by Peter Kahn and his associates relate to the affordances of plants and plant parts (Kahn, Weiss, and Harrington, 2018). These interaction patterns include "climbing high in small tree," "striking wood on wood," "leaning on and hanging from supple tree limbs," "constructing shelter," and "leaning against tree." Each of these patterns includes some form of interaction with trees.

Children seem to have a special affinity for trees. They often mention trees as something they really like to have in places where they play (Laaksoharju and Rappe, 2017). Some children even say they love trees (Argent et al., 2017). Trees appear frequently in children's drawings, and many identify trees as one of their favorite features in a natural environment (Laaksoharju and Rappe, 2017).

☀

Horticultural Therapy

Horticultural therapy, as a form of treatment or intervention, taps into the healing power of plants. This form of therapy is sometimes used with children who live in communities with high poverty and with children who have special needs. One such program, Haven of Green Space in the United Kingdom, is a program for children with behavioral, emotional, and social difficulties (BESD). During a pilot test, thirty-six children with BESD attended monthly horticulture therapy sessions over a six-month period. While activities during the sessions included developing and maintaining gardens on school grounds, the primary focus was on fostering the well-being of students. Assessments showed increases in children's mental health, well-being, and social relationships (Chiumento et al., 2018).

Another horticultural therapy program for children with emotional and/or behavioral problems focused on three activities: flower arranging, planting, and flower pressing. Researchers conducted an experimental study to evaluate the effectiveness of this program in reducing stress and found that children who participated in the program showed a decrease in stress levels in interpersonal relationships, school life, personal problems, and home life (Lee et al., 2018).

Attention Restoration

Plant-rich environments, in addition to being emotionally restorative for children, can also increase their ability to concentrate. This phenomenon—referred to by Rachel Kaplan and Steven Kaplan (1989) as *attention restoration*—has been observed in both typically developing children and children with special needs. Evidence of nature's power for restoring attention has been especially impressive for children with ADHD (van den Berg and van den Berg, 2011).

Schools around the world are recognizing the power of plants in helping children concentrate. Several schools in Amsterdam, the Netherlands, for example, installed green walls (walls filled with plants) in some of their classrooms. Several months later, students in the classrooms with green walls scored better on selective attention measures and rated their classrooms as more attractive than the children in classrooms without a green wall did (van den Berg et al., 2017). Even having plants outside the classroom but within view of the students can reduce student stress and enhance psychological well-being (Li and Sullivan, 2016). Research has found positive links between children's academic performance and trees near schools (Sivarajah, Smith, and Thomas, 2018). These findings apply to different grade levels and to schools in high-poverty areas as well as more advantaged schools (Browing and Rigolon, 2019). Some research suggests that access to trees and other greenness around schools may be especially beneficial for at-risk children (Mitchell et al., 2015) and children with special needs (Ohly et al., 2016).

Promoting Connections between Children and Plants

Many of the benefits of outdoor play for children relate in some way to plants. Plants invite:

- ✿ physical activity: climbing trees, lifting branches, digging holes to plant seeds or seedlings, and so on;
- ✿ scientific exploration: observation, inquiry, experimenting, and so on; and
- ✿ various forms of play: constructive, sociodramatic, risky, and so on.

CONSIDERATIONS AND ADAPTATIONS FOR CHILDREN WITH SPECIAL NEEDS

For gardening activities, raised garden beds—at table height—may be necessary for some children with special needs. A raised bed can accommodate a child in a wheelchair and may be more comfortable for a child who has motor coordination problems. It can also be helpful for children with visual impairments.

For noisy plant-related activities—such as pound art—keep in mind that children with ASD may have a low tolerance for loud noises. Provide a quiet place within the outdoor playspace to give children a place to retreat. Another idea is to provide headphones or a noise-reducing headset for a child with a low tolerance for noise.

With nature play, keep in mind that some children with ASD may be oversensitive to sensory stimulation, such as getting dirty or wet. They may not want to touch rough surfaces, such as the shaggy bark on some trees. Don't try to force sensory stimulation; let the child take the lead. At times, it may be helpful to imitate a child's action by keeping a distance of several feet. You might also use narration to describe what a child is doing: state out loud what the child is doing or attempting to do during explorations. Narration can provide support as well as information related to the child's actions and might be used, for example, to help a child become more aware of cause and effect: "I see you shaking the branch and making the raindrops fall off the leaves."

For more ideas, check out these resources:

Etherington, Natasha. 2012. *Gardening for Children with Autism Spectrum Disorders and Special Educational Needs: Engaging With Nature to Combat Anxiety, Promote Sensory Integration and Build Social Skills.* London, UK: Jessica Kingsley.

Kids Gardening, https://kidsgardening.org

Moore, Robin. 1993. *Plants for Play: A Plant Selection Guide for Children's Outdoor Environments.* Berkeley, CA: MIG Communications.

Winterbottom, Daniel, and Amy Wagenfeld. 2015. *Therapeutic Gardens: Design for Healing Spaces.* Portland, OR: Timber Press.

Plants also provide shade, stimulate the senses, and help establish a calm, relaxing environment.

One of the most obvious ways to promote children's engagement with plants is to provide frequent opportunities for them to experience plant-rich environments. Here are a few more specific ideas.

- ✿ **Garden with children.** Involve children in every aspect of the gardening project: building compost piles, preparing the soil, planting the seed, watering the plants, and harvesting the produce. In addition to learning about plants, gardening will also promote children's sense of wonder, contribute to their self-esteem, foster motor coordination, and deepen their connection with nature. Gardening may represent one of the deepest forms of engagement with nature— to plant a seed is to plant a relationship.

- ✿ **Use plants and plant parts in art activities.** These activities can include drawing, painting, making collages, leaf and bark rubbing, sculpting, and so forth. Squish art and pound art can be especially fun. Squish art involves squeezing or crushing leaves or flower petals to release the pigment, such as rubbing a dandelion flower across a blank sheet of paper. Pound art involves pounding instead of squishing. Arrange some small leaves and flower petals on a blank sheet of paper or cardboard. Cover the arrangement with muslin or cotton fabric. Use a child's hammer or a stone to gently pound the material. Pigment from the plant parts will show up on the cloth.

✿ **Encourage nature play.** Nature play can take the form of digging in sand or dirt, running through a pile of leaves, building a den, climbing a tree, and floating leaves or bark in a stream or pond. Loose plant parts, such as leaves, sticks, acorns, pinecones, and flower petals, make wonderful props for sociodramatic play. Encourage children to use plant props, but also teach them to be mindful of the health of the plants. Picking some flowers is fine; picking all the flowers from a bush may be harmful to the bush and other living things such as birds and insects.

✿ **Promote intimate connections with trees.** You might do this by conducting group activities, such as story time, snack time, and rest time, around a tree. Encourage personal engagement with a tree, including climbing, leaning against a tree, drawing, watering, learning about the animals that live in and around a tree, and naming a tree.

✿ **Encourage children to experience plants through all their sensory modalities.** Call attention to the different sensory features of a plant. How do the different parts of a plant feel? How does the plant smell? What is the shape of the entire plant and individual parts of the plant? What sounds can you hear when you're close to the plant—insects buzzing, birds chirping, leaves rustling, branches rubbing, and so on?

✿ **Engage children in the care of plants.** Caring activities can include watering plants and avoiding harm to vulnerable plants. As they climb trees, children should be careful not to break any branches. To help children avoid overwatering seedlings or other small plants, have them use spray bottles rather than cups or buckets.

✿ **Help children become close observers of plants.** One way to do this is to have the children record the growth of a plant or the changes through the different seasons. Another way is to provide observational tools such as hand lenses or other types of magnifiers. Gazing balls, cameras (real or pretend), and strategically placed benches can also encourage closer observation.

✿ **Be attentive to any "environmental epiphanies" children may have with plants.** Environmental epiphanies involve the experience of awe and may be accompanied by a surprising discovery (Giusti et al., 2018). They are usually experienced during significant nature situations, which can interrupt a child's line of thought, provoke new thinking, and offer overwhelming attraction. An environmental epiphany occurred for one child as he discovered that sprinkling water on dry moss "wakes it up." He watched with wonder as a patch of dry brown matter transformed into soft green moss within a few minutes after he sprinkled it with water. He referred to what he witnessed as "moss magic."

✿ **Walk slowly in the presence of plants.** Respect the way in which both plants and children need time to grow.

Knowing Plants as Kin

Sue Stuart-Smith in *The Well-Gardened Mind* (2020) summarizes some of the research on the benefits of close connections with plants. She discusses how prisoners who tend plants are less likely to re-offend after their release from prison and how senior citizens who garden tend to live longer. She also references studies on the power of plants to help people recover from addiction and depression and to be resilient during times of stress and trauma.

We are also hearing from botanists, ecologists, and plant scientists that plants are intelligent living beings and that they are our kin (Kimmerer, 2013). Plants can keep us company, comfort us, and teach us what it means to live in an interconnected world. We may not think about this every day, but as humans we exist only by the generosity of our plant companions. Young children seem to know this intuitively. It's not unusual for a child to wave back to the leaves on a tree, to say good night to seeds as they're covered with a handful of soil, to express concern for a wilting plant, and to thank a strawberry plant for the fruit it provides. We do well to encourage such activities.

REFERENCES

Argent, Adrienne, et al. 2017. "A Dialogue About Place and Living Pedagogies: Trees, Ferns, Blood, Children, Educators, and Wood Cutters." *Journal of Childhoods and Pedagogies* 1(2): 1–20.

Arvidsen, Jan, and Simon Beames. 2019. "Young Children's Outdoor Refuges: Movements and (Dis) Entanglements." *Children's Geographies* 17(4): 401–412.

Bratman, Gregory N., et al. 2015. "Nature Experience Reduces Rumination and Subgenual Prefrontal Cortex Activation." *PNAS* 112(28): 8567–8572.

Browning, Matthew H.E.M., and Alessandro Rigolon. 2019. "Could Nature Help Children Rise Out of Poverty? Green Space and Future Earnings from a Cohort in Ten U.S. Cities." *Environmental Research* 176: 108449.

Byström, Kristina, Patrik Grahn, and Caroline Hägerhäll. 2019. "Vitality from Experiences in Nature and Contact with Animals—A Way to Develop Joint Attention and Social Engagement in Children with Autism?" *International Journal of Environmental Research and Public Health* 16(23): 4673

Chiumento, Anna, et al. 2018. "A Haven of Green Space: Learning from a Pilot Pre-Post Evaluation of a School-Based Social and Therapeutic Horticulture Intervention with Children." *BMC Public Health* 18: 836.

Cooke, Emma, et al. 2020. "'Lie in the Grass, the Soft Grass': Relaxation Accounts of Young Children Attending Childcare." *Children and Youth Services Review* 109: 104722.

Faber Taylor, Andrea, and Frances E. M. Kuo. 2011. "Could Exposure to Everyday Green Spaces Help Treat ADHD? Evidence from Children's Play Settings." *Applied Psychology: Health and Well-Being* 3(3): 281–303.

Giusti, Matteo, et al. 2018. "A Framework to Assess Where and How Children Connect to Nature." *Frontiers in Psychology* 8: 2283.

Kahn, Peter H., Thea Weiss, and Kit Harrington. 2018. "Modeling Child-Nature Interaction in a Nature Preschool: A Proof of Concept." *Frontiers in Psychology* 9: 835.

Kaplan, Rachel, and Stephen Kaplan. 1989. *The Experience of Nature: A Psychological Perspective.* Cambridge, UK: Cambridge University Press.

Kimmerer, Robin W. 2013. *Braiding Sweetgrass: Indigenous Wisdom, Scientific Knowledge, and the Teachings of Plants.* Minneapolis, MN: Milkweed Editions.

Laaksoharju, Taina, and Erja Rappe. 2017. "Trees as Affordances for Connectedness to Place—A Model to Facilitate Children's Relationship with Nature." *Urban Forestry and Urban Greening* 28: 150–159.

Laaksoharju, Taina, Erja Rappe, and Taina Kaivola. 2012. "Garden Affordances for Social Learning, Play, and for Building Nature-Child Relationship." *Urban Forestry and Urban Greening* 11: 195–203.

Lee, Min Jung, et al. 2018. "A Pilot Study: Horticulture-Related Activities Significantly Reduce Stress and Salivary Cortisol Concentration of Maladjusted Elementary School Children." *Complementary Therapies in Medicine* 37: 172–177.

Li, Dongying, and William C. Sullivan. 2016. "Impact of Views to School Landscapes on Recovery from Stress and Mental Fatigue." *Landscape and Urban Planning* 148: 149–158.

Mitchell, Richard J., et al. 2015. "Neighborhood Environments and Socioeconomic Inequalities in Mental Well-Being." *American Journal of Preventive Medicine* 49(1): 80–84.

Morrissey, Anne-Marie, Caroline Scott, and Mark Rahimi. 2017. "A Comparison of Sociodramatic Play Processes of Preschoolers in a Naturalized and a Traditional Outdoor Space." *International Journal of Play* 6(2): 177–197.

Ohly, Heather, et al. 2016. "A Systematic Review of the Health and Well-Being Impacts of School Gardening: Synthesis of Quantitative and Qualitative Evidence." *BMC Public Health* 16(1): 286.

Sivarajah, Sivajanani, Sandy M. Smith, and Sean C. Thomas. 2018. "Tree Cover and Species Composition Effects on Academic Performance of Primary School Students." *PLOS ONE* 13(2): e0193254. https://doi.org/10.1371/journal.pone.0193254

Stuart-Smith, Sue. 2020. *The Well-Gardened Mind: The Restorative Power of Nature.* New York: Scribner.

Swank, Jacqueline M., and Sondra Smith-Adcock. 2018. "On-Task Behavior of Children with Attention-Deficit/Hyperactivity Disorder: Examining Treatment Effectiveness of Play Therapy Intervention." *International Journal of Play Therapy* 27(4): 187–197.

van den Berg, Agnes, and Clemens van den Berg. 2011. "A Comparison of Children with ADHD in a Natural and Built Setting." *Child: Care, Health and Development* 37(3): 430–439.

van den Berg, Agnes, et al. 2017. "Green Walls for a Restorative Classroom Environment: A Controlled Evaluation Study." *Environment and Behavior* 49(7): 791–813.

Zimanyi, Louise, and Olga Rossovska. 2020. "'Who Is John the Snail and When Can We Meet Him?' Parent Perspectives on Children's Engagement in a Forest Nature Program." *Journal of Innovation in Polytechnic Education.* http://humberpress.com/wp-content/uploads/2020/10/Jipe-Zimanyi-Rossovska-Final.pdf

Final Thoughts

Two thoughts come to mind as I write this final section, one relating to home and kinship and the other to wonder and joy.

When speaking of plants and animals, we might use the word *habitat* in reference to the natural environment in which they normally live. The natural habitat allows these organisms to have what they need to survive and thrive. A particular habitat—such as a forest, desert, or freshwater lake—is home to many different organisms, all interacting with each other in some way. Each organism belongs in that environment. On a larger scale, the entire natural world is home to all earthly living creatures, including humans.

Home is the place where we dwell or abide. If we're fortunate, we develop a positive relationship with the place we live in and feel a sense of kinship with others who share that space with us.

Home is also the place where we belong. *Belonging* is a soulful word. It implies a close or intimate relationship, a kinship. With a sense of belonging, we feel that we fit in or mesh well with those around us. With a sense of belonging, we feel that we are accepted and valued as a contributing member of a group. Unfortunately, not everyone feels this sense of belonging in the places where they live, work, and play.

This book is based on the knowledge that nature is home to us all and that everyone belongs. Yet, we see that certain groups of people—including people in low-income communities, people of color, and people with special needs—are underrepresented in the use of outdoor natural spaces (Alderton et al., 2019). Inequities related to access to nature and its associated benefits do exist and need to be addressed.

This book is also based on the knowledge that nature is a source of wonder and that engagement with nature is a major contributor to quality of life. As adults, our sense of wonder may be somewhat dimmed (Carson, 1956), but young children—if given the chance—experience nature as a magical place. There are certainly times in our adult lives when we still do, too.

One such time occurred for the astronaut Laurel Clark as she traveled through space on the *Columbia* shuttle mission in 2003. Her communications back to Earth included observations about the experiments she did in space with different living organisms. One of her comments related to watching a silkworm hatch from its cocoon while in orbit. Laurel described the experience to a reporter: "There was a moth in there, and it still had its wings crumpled up, and it was just starting to pump its wings up. Life continues in lots of places, and life is a magical thing" (CNN, 2003).

Clark and her fellow crew members died when *Columbia* disintegrated during re-entry. As tragic as her story is, it can remind us of the wonder and magic of nature. It can also remind us of how important it is to witness and treasure the beauty of nature here on Earth, to find joy in it, and to make sure that all children have the opportunity to experience the many benefits nature has to offer.

A group of young children were once asked to describe an ideal place to play. One child in a wheelchair said she wanted a playspace with a tree house—but one that she could get into. As challenging as that might seem, creative planners have figured out how to make a wheelchair-accessible tree house. With enough caring and vision, we can make nature more accessible to all children. The benefits children can gain from deep engagement with nature are too great to be dismissed. The time to ensure that every child has access to nature is now. We can do this.

REFERENCES

Alderton, Amanda, et al. 2019. "Reducing Inequities in Early Childhood Mental Health: How Might the Neighborhood Built Environment Help Close the Gap? A Systematic Search and Critical Review." *International Journal of Environmental Research and Public Health* 16(9): 1516.

Carson, Rachel. 1956. *The Sense of Wonder*. New York: Harper and Rowe.

CNN. 2003. "Astronaut Clark: 'Life Is a Magical Thing.'" CNN. https://www.cnn.com/2003/US/02/01/sprj.colu.profile.clark/index.html

Contributors

Sally Anderson, MA

Founder-Director-Lead Teacher SOL Forest School, Tijeras, NM

https://www.solforestschool.com/

Early Childhood Coordinator, Nature Niños New Mexico

https://www.natureninos.org/certification-program/

Sally has worked for more than thirty years with young children from a variety of backgrounds and abilities. For the last decade, she has collaborated closely with the Natural World to bring natural loose-parts play into early childhood centers while also bringing children out regularly to learn through school gardening, walking field trips, nature play, and forest school–inspired programming. She is the course facilitator for the Nature Niños Wonder-lings course, a yearlong online Nature and Place-Based Early Childhood Education entry-level training program for teachers of young children who wish to use nature as an ally in their teaching.

Patti Bailie, PhD

Associate Professor of Early Childhood Education, University of Maine at Farmington

Patti has worked in the field of early childhood environmental education for thirty years. She served as founding director of the Schlitz Audubon Nature Center Preschool in Milwaukee, Wisconsin; as codirector of the Early Childhood Outdoors Institute at the Fontenelle Nature Association in Omaha, Nebraska; and as an educator at the Nature Center at Shaker Lakes in Cleveland, Ohio. She was also the assistant director of the Nature-Based Early Childhood Education Certificate program at Antioch University New England, teaching the first course on nature-based early childhood curriculum. She now works with preservice teachers, integrating nature-based experiences in the teacher-preparation program.

Kathryn Hunt Baker, MEd

Katie has worked in the field of early childhood education for more than a decade and has a passion for emergent curriculum and play-based learning. She is a nature-based educator and consultant who earned a master's of education in Foundations of Education and a master's certificate in Nature-Based Education. She owned and operated The Neighborhood Playroom, a nature-based daycare program in Leicester, Massachusetts, and is currently working for Turn Back Time, a farm and nature-based program in Paxton, Massachusetts.

Marilyn Brink, MEd

Marilyn is an early childhood educator, nature-play advocate, and passionate facilitator of nature-based early learning, Understanding the important role early childhood educators hold in the lives and learning of young children, Marilyn helps educators understand access to nature as an issue of justice, equity, diversity, and inclusion. She has helped Head Start programs re-imagine children's access to nature in urban settings where they often lack safe access to parks. Most recently, she led a professional-development program for informal educators who work with young children at zoos, aquariums, nature centers, and other nature-based settings.

Laura Brothwell

Architect and Pedagogista of Stone Hen

https://www.stonehen.co.uk/

Imaginator and Cofounder of the Early Years International Academy

https://www.earlyyearsinternational.com/

Laura supports local, national, and global initiatives to connect children back to their roots and rediscover the joys of childhood.

Lisa Burris

Lisa and her husband, Jim, have raised six children, three of whom have special needs. It was through her children that Lisa first recognized the fantastic effects that nature has as a great equalizer and healer, inspiring her to begin Turn Back Time, a nature-based education program for children of all abilities. She earned a master's certificate in Nature-Based Education from Antioch University. She has worked with children as an applied behavior therapist, taught preschool- and school-aged children for eight years, and is a trained foster parent for the Commonwealth of Massachusetts.

Huan Chen, PhD

Huan is cofounder of the Early Years International Academy and has 23,000 followers of her professional blog in China. She actively promotes nature- and play-based education through teacher training, consulting, writing, and translating. She has translated two inspiring books: *Nature and Young Children: Encouraging Creative Play and Learning in Natural Environments* by Dr. Ruth Wilson and *Can I Go and Play Now? Rethinking the Early Years* by Greg Bottrill.

Sylvia Collazo, PhD

Sylvia has a doctorate in exceptional student education (special education) from Florida Atlantic University, where she specialized in early childhood. Her dissertation focused on the effects of professional development that she created on nature-based teaching strategies for early childhood educators of children with developmental disabilities. Driven by her personal experiences as a sibling of a now-adult with special needs, Sylvia has spent nearly twenty years serving children with disabilities, their families, and fellow educators in a variety of roles, including early childhood special education teacher, inclusion specialist, behavior therapist, and consultant.

Sandra Duncan, EdD

Working to assure the miracle and magic of childhood through indoor and outdoor classroom environments that are designed intentionally to connect young children to their classrooms, communities, and neighborhoods, Sandra is an international consultant, author of six books focused on the environmental design of early childhood classrooms, and designer of a preschool furniture collection called Sense of Place.

Beth Frankel, LSW-MA

Owner/Operator of The Care Farm, LLC

https://www.thecarefarmnh.com/

Beth has practiced social work with both youth and adults for eighteen years. Through her experience with a variety of population groups, she became aware of the many benefits that animals and nature had on her clients' physical and mental health and well-being. She opened The Care Farm, LLC, in Hollis, New Hampshire, in 2016.

Carie Green, PhD

https://sites.google.com/alaska.edu/eidproject/project-overview

Carie earned her doctorate in education from the University of Wyoming in 2011. She currently serves as an associate professor and endowed director of early childhood education and outreach at South Dakota State University. Her research expertise revolves around the emotional and behavioral attributes of children's place and environmental identity development and participatory research methods with young children. She is the author of *Children's Environmental Identity Development*.

Christine Kiewra, MA

Christine is an assistant professor of practice at the University of Nebraska–Lincoln in the Department of Child, Youth, and Family Studies. She has more than twenty years of experience in early childhood care and education, teaching in the classroom, collaborating with families, coaching and providing professional development for teachers, and as a program administrator. She earned a master of arts in special education, is a World Forum Foundation Global Leader for Young Children, coordinates the Bridging Research and Practice column in *Exchange Magazine*, and is on the board of consulting editors for the *International Journal of Early Childhood Environmental Education*.

Helen McDonald, MA

Helen serves as the pedagogical director for the Collaborative Teachers Institute and as center director and teacher at La Casita Parent Cooperative Preschool, both in Santa Fe, New Mexico.

Mariam Murphy

Mariam is the Youth and Family Programs Inclusion Coordinator at The Morton Arboretum in Lisle, Illinois. As a special educator with a love of outdoor exploration, her focus has become providing opportunities for individuals with special needs to connect with nature.

Anne Ouwerkerk

Anne is an early childhood educator who has worked with children in a variety of settings for more than thirty years. Her passion is to learn in and from nature with young children. She recently completed a graduate certificate in Nature Based Early Childhood Education, and she has introduced nature-based learning to public preschool programs. She is passionate about creating inclusive outdoor classrooms.

Tiffany Pearsall, MA

Executive Director, Lead Teacher, Founder at Play Frontier, Stabler, Washington

Tiffany has worked in early childhood education since graduating in 2010. She formed Play Frontier, a full-day, fully licensed nature playschool for children from birth to five in 2018. She is a play advocate for grown-ups and littles alike and strives to treat adult learners with the same respect she gives the children in her care. In addition to playing in the woods with her class, Tiffany mentors new teachers and programs, hosts podcasts, and creates professional- development trainings on all things play and nature.

Jane Piselli, MEd

Summer Camp Director and Preschool Teacher, New Canaan Nature Center, New Canaan, Connecticut

Jane graduated from Antioch University New England with a master's in education as well as a certification in early childhood, special education, and elementary teaching. They also have their certificate in Nature-Based Preschool. Jane's passion is getting out of the classroom and exploring the outdoors. Jane believes that, by providing children with real experiences and time to explore the world around them and their own development as humans, they will fall in love with the world of learning. Jane believes deeply in early intervention and is convinced that outdoor schools are the best natural start we can give all children across the ability spectrum.

Sheila Williams Ridge

Sheila is the director of the Shirley G. Moore Lab School at the University of Minnesota. She has a bachelor's degree in biology and master's degree in education, as well as experience as a business manager and preschool teacher and naturalist. She is a facilitator for the NAEYC Young Children and Nature Interest Forum, serves on the Voices and Choices coalition, is a board member for the Minneapolis Nature Preschool, is a board member for Dodge Nature Center, and is a member of the Natural Start Alliance Council. She is coauthor of the book *Nature-Based Learning for Young Children: Anytime, Anywhere, on Any Budget* and is passionate about encouraging nature-based play and the lasting developmental benefits of a relationship between children and nature.

Nancy Rosenow

Nancy is founder and chief executive officer of the nonprofit Dimensions Educational Research Foundation, whose mission is to inspire joy and wonder in children, educators, and communities with a heart-centered approach to early education. Her work supports the major departments of the Foundation: The Nature Explore Program, Exchange Press, Dimensions Research Initiative, and Dimensions Education Programs. She serves as an administrative partner of the World Forum Foundation on Early Care and Education and is a founding member of its Nature Action Collaborative for Children. She has served as a guest editor of a special edition on the Greening of Early Childhood Programs for the research journal *Children, Youth and Environments*. She is the author of *Heart-Centered Teaching Inspired by Nature* and coauthor of *Learning with Nature* and *Growing with Nature*.

Jennifer Rosinia, PhD, OTR/L

Jennifer is an occupational therapist and child development specialist. She has a special interest in the neurosciences, specifically sensory processing, the influence that stress and adverse experiences have on the developing child, as well as social emotional learning and the importance of relationships. She is a senior instructor at the Erikson Institute and has also taught courses and lectured at several colleges and universities in the Chicago area. She is the president of Kid Links Unlimited, Inc., a company whose mission is to link theory to practice, families with professionals, and children with their optimal potential.

Deborah Schein, PhD

http://growingwonder.com/

Deb has been an early childhood educator since 1972 and earned her doctorate in early childhood education in 2012 with a focus on spiritual development. She teaches at Champlain College and provides professional development for MN Develop/Achieve. She is an author of two books on spirituality and continues to research the relationship between spiritual development, nature, play, peace, and well-being. She serves on the editing team of a new journal titled *Soul to Soul* and is creating a local art-rock garden in her community to strengthen the relationship between spirituality and nature.

Patty Born Selly, EdD

Patty is an assistant professor of environmental and STEM education and is director of Hamline's master's degree program in natural science and environmental education. A former wildlife rehabilitator who has worked in classroom settings throughout her career, she has served as a fire technician, a wildlife/animal-care technician, and a museum educator. Patty has authored three books for educators on the importance of nature and animals in early childhood education. Her research includes multispecies relations, urban environmental education for early learners, and equity and inclusion in environmental and STEM education.

Marisa Soboleski
New Mexico School for the Deaf Forest Day Learning Leader/Educator

Marisa is a deaf mother to two children, one of whom is deafblind, the other a hearing CODA (child of deaf adult). In her work, she coordinates and creates an inquiry-based and experiential approach to education with a focus on socio-emotional development and learning in a nature and place-based setting for children who are deaf and deaf-disabled. She has more than ten years of experience in facilitating and holding dialogues in nature and social-justice education. Marisa and her family enjoy all things about nature: camping, paddling on the river, long walks with their dogs, gardening, wild foraging, and tending to their small farm.

Rachel Tenney

Rachel is an early childhood special-education teacher in New York City with a strong interest in integrating nature-based experiences in their work with young children. They have a master's degree in early childhood general and special education from Bank Street College of Education and a certificate in nature-based early childhood education from Antioch University New England. Rachel recently launched Robins & Roots, an inclusive nature-based program for preschoolers and early elementary students in Prospect Park, Brooklyn, New York.

Nora Thompson, MA

Nora has worked for more than forty years in early childhood education, most of it in inclusive special-education public school settings in Michigan. She has worked as an early childhood special-education teacher and as a director of a municipal child-care center, and she established a Reggio-inspired inclusive early childhood center. She was a teacher educator at Michigan State University and is now a peer-review coordinator and issue editor for *Innovations in Early Education: The International Reggio Emilia Exchange* and a program associate of the North American Reggio Emilia Alliance.

Angela Wildermuth

https://urbanwildstl.com/

Angela is the founder, director, and lead teacher of Wilderkids Urban Forest School in St. Louis, Missouri. Wilderkids offers child-led, play-based, and nature-immersive classes during the school year for preschool and early-elementary children. She is the founder of Wildercamp, which offers play-based, forest-school inspired, mixed-age summer camps in local parks in the St. Louis area. She serves as a nature play consultant for Play-MO, a volunteer playwork organization based in St. Louis.

Meixi Yan

Meixi is currently working toward her master's degree at the Institute of Education, University College London. She served as a volunteer teacher in Qingchuan Post-disaster Reconstruction Primary School and Lhasa-Tibet Middle School. Now she is committed to delivering nature-based education and integrating general education into daily life.

Xi Yang

Xi has completed a three-year Waldorf education training and has been working with children for seven years. She has rich experience in working with children with special needs. She believes educators should accompany children's journey of development with tenderness and care.

Xiuping Yang

Xiuping is the founder of Dali Yuanshan Academy. She graduated from Nanjing Special Education Teachers College in 2014, majoring in child rehabilitation and autism, and has been engaged in special education since graduation.

Gigi Schroeder Yu, PhD

Assistant Professor in Art Education, University of New Mexico

Gigi has more than twenty years of visual arts teaching experience with children and adults in community settings, museums, higher education, and public-school classrooms in Arizona, Illinois, Wisconsin, and New Mexico. Gigi worked with the New Mexico Wildlife Federation Nature Niños Wonder-lings, Albuquerque Art Museum, the Santa Fe Opera Early Childhood Initiative, the Albuquerque Public Schools Office of Early Childhood, and Chicago Artist Partners in Education providing pedagogical leadership and facilitating professional development, with an emphasis on early childhood art education. Currently, she is also editor for the journal *Innovations in Early Education: The International Reggio Emilia Exchange*.

Shiqi Yue

Shiqi works in Tongmai Kindergarten in Huangshi City, China. She has been engaged in preschool education for six years, with a high interest in the behavioral psychology of young children. Since 2020, she has been inspired by Dr. Huan Chen's training to practice early education in the natural environment.

Index